ماهوالإســـلام

What is Islam

© **Maktaba Dar-us-Salam, 2002**
King Fahd National Library Cataloging-in-Publication Data
Darussalam
What is Islam-Riyadh.
104p., 14x21 cm.
ISBN 9960-861-71-4
I- Islam General-Principles   II-Title
210. dc.   2819/23
Legal Deposit no. 2819/23
ISBN 9960-861-71-4

HEAD OFFICE

P.O. Box: 22743, Riyadh 11416 K.S.A.Tel: 00966-01-4033962/4043432 Fax: 4021659
E-mail: Riyadh@dar-us-salam.com, darussalam@awalnet.net.sa Website: www.dar-us-salam.com

K.S.A. **Darussalam Showrooms:**
  Riyadh
Olaya branch: Tel 00966-1-4614483 Fax: 4644945
Malaz branch: Tel 4735220 Fax: 4735221
* **Jeddah**
  Tel: 00966-2-6879254 Fax: 6336270
* **Al-Khobar**
  Tel: 00966-3-8692900 Fax: 00966-3-8691551
U.A.E
* **Darussalam, Sharjah U.A.E**
  Tel: 00971-6-5632623 Fax: 5632624
  Sharjah@dar-us-salam.com
PAKISTAN
* **Darussalam, 36 B Lower Mall, Lahore**
  Tel: 0092-42-724 0024 Fax: 7354072
  Lahore@dar-us-salam.com
* Rahman Market, Ghazni Street
  Urdu Bazar Lahore
  Tel: 0092-42-7120054 Fax: 7320703
U.S.A
* **Darussalam, Houston**
  P.O Box: 79194 Tx 77279
  Tel: 001-713-722 0419 Fax: 001-713-722 0431
  E-mail: Webmaster@dar-us-salam.com
* **Darussalam, New York** 186 Atlantic Ave, Brooklyn
  New York-11217, Tel: 001-718-625 5925
  Fax: 718-625 1511
  Email: darussalamny@hotmail.com
U.K
* **Darussalam International Publications Ltd.**
  Leyton Business Centre
  Unit – 17, Etloe Road, Leyton, London, E10 7BT
  Tel: 00 44 20 8539 4885 Fax: 00 44 20 8539 4889
  Mobile: 00 44 7947 306 706
* **Darussalam International Publications Limited**
  146 Park Road,
  London NW8 7RG Tel: 00 44 20 725 2246
* **Darussalam**
  398-400 Coventry Road, Small Heath
  Birmingham, B10 0UF
  Tel: 0121 77204792 Fax: 0121 772 4345
  E-mail: info@darussalamuk.com
  Web: www.darussalamuk.com

FRANCE
* Editions & Librairie Essalam
  135, Bd de Ménilmontant- 75011 Paris
  Tél: 0033-01- 43 38 19 56/ 44 83
  Fax: 0033-01- 43 57 44 31
  E-mail: essalam@essalam.com
AUSTRALIA
* ICIS: Ground Floor 165-171, Haldon St.
  Lakemba NSW 2195, Australia
  Tel: 00612 9758 4040 Fax: 9758 4030
MALAYSIA
* E&D Books SDN. BHD.-321 B 3rd Floor,
  Suria Klcc
  Kuala Lumpur City Center 50088
  Tel: 00603-21663433
  Fax: 00603-42573758
  E-mail: endbook@tm.net.my
SINGAPORE
* Muslim Converts Association of Singapore
  32 Onan Road The Galaxy Singapore- 424484
  Tel: 0065-440 6924, 348 8344
  Fax: 440 6724
SRI LANKA
* Darul Kitab 6, Nimal Road, Colombo-4
  Tel: 0094-1-589 038 Fax: 0094-74 722433
KUWAIT
* Islam Presentation Committee
  Enlightment Book Shop
  P.O. Box: 1613, Safat 13017 Kuwait
  Tel: 00965-244 7526, Fax: 240 0057
INDIA
* Islamic Dimensions
  56/58 Tandel Street (North)
  Dongri, Mumbai 4000 009,India
  Tel: 0091-22-3736875, Fax: 3730689
  E-mail:sales@IRF.net
SOUTH AFRICA
* Islamic Da´wah Movement (IDM)
  48009 Qualbert 4078 Durban,South Africa
  Tel: 0027-31-304-6883
  Fax: 0027-31-305-1292
  E-mail: idm@ion.co.za

WHAT IS ISLAM

Compiled by
Research Division Darussalam

Published by
DARUSSALAM
Publishers & Distributors
Riyadh, Saudi Arabia

In the Name of Allâh,
the Most Gracious, the Most Marciful

"And I (Allâh) created not the jinn and mankind except that they should worship Me (Alone). I seek not any provision from them (i.e. provision for themselves or for My creatures) nor do I ask that they should feed Me (i.e. feed themselves or My creatures). Verily, Allâh is the All-Provider, Owner of Power, the Most Strong. And verily, for those who do wrong, there is a portion of torment like the evil portion of torment (which came for) their likes (of old); so let them not ask Me to hasten on! Then woe to those who disbelieve (in Allâh and His Oneness – Islamic Monotheism) from their Day which they have been promised (for their punishment)." [1]

(*Sûrah Adh-Dhâriyât*, 51: 56-60)

---

[1]   Narrated Anas ﷺ: The Prophet ﷺ said, "Allâh will say to the person of the (Hell) Fire who will receive the least punishment, 'If you had everything on the earth, would you give it as a ransom to free yourself (i.e., save yourself from this Fire)?" He will say, 'Yes.' Then Allâh will say, 'While you were in the backbone of Adam, I asked you much less than this, (i.e., not to worship others besides Me), but you insisted on worshipping others besides Me." (*Shaih Al-Bukhari*, *Hadith* No. 3334)

Contents

A Note from the Publisher

This religion – Islam is a heavenly system (or regime) for all the dwellers of the earth, and it is a mighty treasure if only mankind realizes its authenticity and truth. And in what a great need the whole world is today for real understanding and thorough studying of its rules and regulations – i.e., the Noble Qur'ân and the pious *Sunnah* (legal ways, etc.) of the Prophet Muhammad ﷺ, as these (the Qur'ân and *As-Sunnah*) accede to the demand of the people to know their Creator (the Almighty Allâh, the Blessed, the Most High), organize and regulate the relations between them on the foundations of (Godly) Divine Justice and equality and respond to the human nature equally to that which makes sure for them their welfare (happiness) in this world and in the Hereafter (after their deaths).

And how many disasters, calamities and wars, the mankind of the whole world is suffering because of their differences in their faith, and organizations, which have broken them into the worst type of breaking, so there remains no way out for any security or any safety or any peace except with Islam, i.e., by putting in practice the Laws of their Creator, Allâh, (i.e., the Qur'ân and *As-Sunnah*).

Invitation to this religion – Islam is incumbent upon all those who have known it, and have enjoyed its taste and have been guided through its guidance. In fact it is a great responsibility and a trust (of Allâh) over (the shoulders of) all those who know Islam, to preach it to mankind and invite them to it in a language which they speak and understand.

Introduction

Allâh's Statement

(The Noble Qur'ân, Verses 3: 19, 20 –
translated by Al-Hilali and Khan)

"Truly, the religion with Allâh is Islam. Those who were given the Scripture (Jews and Christians) did not differ except out of mutual jealousy, after knowledge had come to them. And whoever disbelieves in the *Ayât* (proofs, evidences, verses, signs, revelations, etc.) of Allâh, then surely Allâh is Swift in calling to account. So, if they dispute with you (Muhammad ﷺ), say: 'I have submitted myself to Allâh (in Islam), and (so have) those who follow me.' And say to those who were given the Scripture (Jews and Christians) and to those who are illiterates (Arab pagans): 'Do you (also) submit yourselves (to Allâh in Islam)?' If they do, they are rightly guided; but if they turn away, your duty is only to convey the Message; and Allâh is All-Seer of (His) slaves."

Who is Allâh?

'Allâh, is the proper name applied to the True God, Who exists Alone, and includes all His Excellent Divine Names and Perfect Attributes. Allâh ﷻ is One and Unique. He has no son, partner or equal. As Allâh says in the Noble Qur'ân:

"And they attribute falsely without knowledge sons and daughters to Him. He is Glorified and Exalted above all that (evil) they attribute to Him. He is the Originator of the heavens and the earth. How can He have children when He has no wife? He created all things and He is the All-Knower of everything.[1] Such is Allâh, your Lord! *Lâ ilâha illa Huwa*

---

[1] Narrated Ibn 'Abbâs رضى الله عنهما : The Prophet ﷺ said that Allâh said, "The son of Adam tells lies against Me though he has no right to do so, and he abuses Me though he has no right to do so. As for his telling lies against Me, he claims that I cannot re-create him as I created him before; and as for his abusing Me: it is his statement that I have a son (or offspring). No! Glorified I am! I am far from taking a wife or a son (or offspring). " (*Sahih Al-Bukhâri, Hadîth* No. 4482)

(none has the right to be worshipped but He), the Creator of all things. So worship Him (Alone), and He is the *Wakîl* (Trustee, Disposer of affairs or Guardian) over all things. No vision can grasp Him, but He grasps all vision. He is *Al-Latîf* (the Most Subtle and Courteous), the Well-Acquainted (with all things)." (V. 6:100-103)

He is the Sole Creator and Sustainer of the universe. Every creature bears witness to His Oneness, Divinity and Lordship *Rubûbiyah*[1] as well as to the uniqueness of His Attributes and Names. His Essence does not resemble any other essence. There is none like Him. He is the One. He is the Lord without Whom no affairs are accomplished, and to Whom Lordship ultimately belongs. He neither begets nor is begotten. He is not inherent in anything, nor is anything inherent in Him. All creatures stand in need of Him, yet He stands in need of none. Allâh ﷻ is the Omnipotent and the Omniscient, the One Whose knowledge comprehends in the most perfect manner, all things, hidden or manifest. But He is the Most Great.

Allâh ﷻ, the Supreme, is the Lord of everything, Who disposes all affairs. He is the Most Merciful; One Whose mercy is boundless and encompasses everything. He is far removed from injustice and tyranny. His justice ensures order in the universe where nothing is out of order. There is no one to share His dominion, nor does He take a helper or supporter from His creatures. He is the Lord of the *'Alamîn* (mankind, jinn and all that exists).

He is above the seven heavens, and rose over His Throne in the manner that suits His Majesty. As Allâh says in the Noble Qur'ân:

"The Most Gracious (Allâh) rose over *(Istawâ)* the (Mighty) Throne (in a manner that suits His Majesty). To

---

[1] *Rubûbiyah*: Lordship is *Rubûbiyah* in Arabic. It derives from *Rabb*. There is no proper equivalent for *Rabb* in the English language. It means the One and the Only Lord for all the universe, its Creator, Owner, Organizer, Provider, Master, Planner, Sustainer, Cherisher, and Giver of security. *Rabb* is also one of the Names of Allâh.

Him belongs all that is in the heavens and all that is on the earth, and all that is between them, and all that is under the soil. And if you (O Muhammad ﷺ) speak (the invocation) aloud, then verily, He knows the secret and that which is yet more hidden. Allâh! *Lâ ilâha illa Huwa* (none has the right to be worshipped but He)! To Him belong the Best Names." (V. 20: 5-8)

"They made not a just estimate of Allâh such as is due to Him. And on the Day of Resurrection the whole of the earth will be grasped by His Hand[1] and the heavens will be rolled up in His Right Hand. Glorified is He, and High is He above all that they associate as partners with Him!" (V. 39:67)

---

[1]   Narrated Abû Hurairah ﷺ: I heard Allâh's Messenger ﷺ saying, "(On the Day of Resurrection) Allâh will grasp the whole planet of earth (by His Hand), and roll all the heavens up with His Right Hand, and then He will say, 'I am the King; where are the kings of the earth?'" (*Sahih Al-Bukhari, Hadîth* No. 4812)

"Allâh! *Lâ ilâha illa Huwa* (none has the right to be worshipped but He), *Al-Hayyul-Qayyum* (the Ever Living, the One Who sustains and protects all that exists). Neither slumber nor sleep overtakes Him. To Him belongs whatever is in the heavens and whatever is on the earth. Who is he that can intercede with Him except with His Permission? He knows what happens to them (His creatures) in this world, and what will happen to them in the Hereafter. And they will never encompass anything of His Knowledge except that which He wills. His *Kursî* extends over the heavens and the earth, and He feels no fatigue in guarding and preserving them. And He is the Most High, the Most Great. [This Verse 2:255, is called *Ayat-ul-Kursî*.]

"And He is Allâh: *Lâ ilâha illa Huwa* (none has the right to be worshipped but He), His are all praise and thanks (both) in the first (i.e. in this world) and in the last (i.e. in the Hereafter). And for Him is the Decision, and to Him shall you (all) be returned. Say (O Muhammad ﷺ): 'Tell me! If Allâh made the night continuous for you till the Day of Resurrection, which *ilâh* (a god) besides Allâh could bring you light? Will you not then hear?' Say (O Muhammad ﷺ): 'Tell me! If Allâh made the day continuous for you till the Day of Resurrection, which *ilâh* (a god) besides Allâh could bring you night wherein you rest? Will you not then see?' It is out of His Mercy that He has made for you the night and the day that you may rest therein (i.e. during the night) and that you may seek of His Bounty (i.e. during the day) and in order that you may be grateful. And (remember) the Day when He (your Lord – Allâh) will call to them (those who worshipped others along with Allâh), and will say: 'Where are My (so-called) partners, whom you used to assert?' And We shall take out from every nation a witness, and We shall say: 'Bring your proof.' Then they shall know that the truth is with Allâh (Alone), and the lies (false gods) which they invented will disappear from them." (28: 70-75)

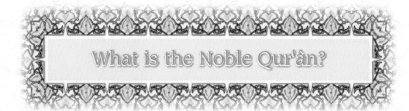

What is the Noble Qur'ân?

The 'Qur'ân' is the Speech of Allâh ﷻ. It is not a creation. It was delivered by the angel Gabriel to Muhammad ﷺ, who would memorize the Verses he received, recite them to the Companions who happened to be with him and order them to write them down immediately. Muhammad ﷺ used to keep a copy of the revealed portions in his house. It is the last of Allâh's Books, which was revealed in installments over a period of twenty-three years. It is divided into 114 *Surah* (Chapters) of unequal length. It is one of the fundamental sources of Islamic teachings. Some of its Chapters and Verses were revealed in Makkah, and the rest were revealed in Al-Madinah. The

Makkan Chapters and Verses are concerned mainly with basic issues of *Aqeedah* (belief) such as monotheism, the signs of the existence of Allâh ﷻ , Resurrection, the life after death and the Day of Resurrection. The Islamic Religion or Belief emphasize on the Oneness of Allâh ﷻ the focal point of the messages with which Allâh ﷻ sent all Prophets and Messengers to mankind, beginning with Adam and ending with Muhammad ﷺ. The  Chapters revealed in Al-Madinah are concerned with acts of worship and actions related to all aspects of life.

Authenticity of the Noble Qur'ân

Muslims are commanded to recite during the day and night and also in their daily prayers and refer all their disputes to it for final judgment. The Qur'ân was compiled at a time when those who had committed it to memory during the lifetime of the Prophet ﷺ were still alive. Allâh ﷻ has promised to preserve it, as He says in the Noble Qur'ân:

"Verily, We, it is We Who have sent down the *Dhikr* (i.e. the Qur'ân) and surely We will guard it (from corruption)." (V. 15:9)

This Verse is a challenge to mankind and everyone is obliged to believe in the miracles of this Qur'ân. It is a clear fact that more than 1400 years have elapsed and not a single word of this Qur'ân has been changed, although the disbelievers tried their utmost to change it in every way, but they failed miserably in their efforts. As it is mentioned in this holy Verse: "We will guard it." By Allâh! He has guarded it. On the contrary, all the other holy Books [the Taurât (Torah), the Injîl (Gospel) have been corrupted in the form of additions or subtractions or alterations in the original text.

It will be so preserved until the Day of Resurrection. Muslims today read and recite the Qur'ânic text that was read and recited during the lifetime of the Prophet Muhammad ﷺ and his Companions. Not a single letter has been added to the Qur'ân or deleted from it. After having examined the Qur'ân, Dr. Maurice Bucaille concluded:

> "Thanks to its undisputed authenticity, the text of the Qur'ân holds a unique place among the Books of Revelation."[1]

The Qur'ân as a Miracle

Allâh the Exalted has challenged Arabs and non-Arabs to produce a Qur'ân similar to the Divine one. The challenge was reduced to ten Chapters, as Allâh says in the Noble Qur'ân:

> "Or they say, 'He (Prophet Muhammad ﷺ) forged it (the Qur'ân).' Say: 'Bring you then ten forged Sûrahs (chapters) like to it, and call whomsoever you can, other than Allâh (to your help), if you speak the truth!' If then they answer you not, know then that it [the Revelation (this Qur'ân)] is sent down with the Knowledge of Allâh and that Lâ ilâha illa Huwa (none has the right to be worshipped but He)! Will you then be Muslims (those who submit in Islam)?" (V.11: 13,14)

And yet they failed to do so. Finally, Allâh challenged them to produce a single forged chapter like unto it. As Allâh ﷻ says:

---

[1] Dr. Maurice Bucaille is a surgeon who has taken great interest in the scientific aspects of the Qur'ân. He learnt Arabic and managed to study the Qur'ân in its original text. He was amazed with its precise scientific data.

"And this Qur'ân is not such as could ever be produced by other than Allâh (Lord of the heavens and the earth), but it is a confirmation of (the Revelation) which was before it [i.e. the Taurât (Torah), and the Injîl (Gospel)], and a full explanation of the Book (i.e. The laws decreed for mankind) – wherein there is no doubt – from the Lord of the *'Alamîn* (mankind, jinn, and all that exists). Or do they say: 'He (Muhammad ﷺ) has forged it?' Say: 'Bring then a *Sûrah* (chapter) like to it, and call upon whomsoever you can besides Allâh, if you are truthful!'" (V. 10: 37, 38)

Although the Arabs at that time were the masters of eloquence and rhetoric, they were incapable of taking up the challenge. They realized that it could never be from other than Allâh ﷻ, the Lord of the *'Alamîn* (mankind, jinn and all that exists).

The difference between the miracles of the previous Messengers, miracles proving their veracity, and that of Allâh's Messenger ﷺ, is that theirs were effective during their lifetime, whereas his miracle of the Qur'ân has remained and will remain effective, everlasting, and unchallenged until the Day of Resurrection. The following are the sayings of Prophet Muhammad ﷺ in this regard:

Narrated Abu Hurairah ﷺ: The Prophet ﷺ said, "There was no Prophet among the Prophets but was given miracles because of which people had security or had belief, but what I have been given is the Divine Revelation which Allâh has revealed to me. So, I hope that my followers will be more than those of any other Prophet on the Day of Resurrection." (*Sahih Al-Bukhari*, Hadith No. 7274)

Narrated Jâbir رضي الله عنهما Some angels came to the Prophet (Muhammad ﷺ) while he was sleeping. Some of them said,

"He is sleeping." Others said, "His eyes are sleeping but his heart is awake." One of them said, "Then set forth an example for him." One of them said, "He is sleeping." Another said, "His eyes are sleeping but his heart is awaking." Then they said, "His example is that of a man who built a house and then offered therein a banquet and sent an inviter (messenger) to invite the people. So, whoever accepted the invitation of the inviter, entered the house and ate of the banquet, and whoever did not accept the invitation of the inviter, did not enter the house, nor did he eat of the banquet." Then the angels said, "Interpret this parable to him so that he may understand it." One of them said, "He is sleeping." The other said, "His eyes are sleeping but his heart is awake." And then they said, "The house stands for Paradise and the call-maker is Muhammad ﷺ; and whoever obeys Muhammad ﷺ, obeys Allâh; and whoever disobeys Muhammad ﷺ, disobeys Allâh. Muhammad ﷺ separated the people (i.e., through his message, the good is distinguished from the bad, and the believers from the disbelievers)." (*Sahih Al-Bukhari, Hadith* No. 7281)

Narrated Abu Hurairah ﷺ: Allâh's Messenger ﷺ said:

"Both in this world and in the Hereafter, I am the nearest of all the people to 'Îsâ (Jesus), the son of Maryam (Mary). The Prophets are paternal brothers; their mothers are different, but their religion is one (i.e., Islamic Monotheism)." (*Sahih Al-Bukhari, Hadith* No. 3443)

Narrated Abu Hurairah ﷺ: Allâh's Messenger ﷺ said: "By Him (Allâh) in Whose Hand Muhammad's soul is, there is none from amongst the Jews and the Christians (of these present nations) who hears about me and then dies without believing

in the Message with which I have been sent (i.e. Islâmic Monotheism), but he will be from the dwellers of the (Hell) Fire." (*Sahih Muslim*, the Book of Faith, Vol. 1, *Hadith* No. 240)

The Qur'ân as a Comprehensive Legislation

The Qur'ân constitutes the most comprehensive concept of Islam on the practical level, as *Shari'ah* (the source of the Divine Laws). It is comprehensive because it includes law as well as moral principles and the Islamic Belief to which every Muslim must subscribe. The Islamic *Shari'ah* is not only suitable for Muslims, but for all mankind at all times. Islamic Laws govern all human acts, by delineating every person's public and private duties toward Allâh and other people.

Man-made laws are subject to alteration and are based on theories. Whenever a new body of legislators assumes authority or a new theory appears and appeals to them, laws are changed accordingly. Divine legislation, on the other hand, is unalterable and perpetual because the One Who authored it is the Everliving and the Everlasting. He is the Creator Who created humans and ordained for them what would suit their needs until the end of time. For this reason, the Qur'ân, being the last Revelation to the last of the Prophets and Messengers, cancels all previous Scriptures.

Many prophecies in the Qur'ân are fulfilled to the letter. Allâh promised those who believe and do good works that He will

surely make them victorious on earth. They ruled a vast land encompassing many countries in the world.

Science and the Noble Qur'ân

Muhammad was unlettered. He could neither read nor write, and he grew up in Makkah where there were no schools. He was far away from the scientific circles that existed in Syria, Alexandria, Athens or Rome. Moreover, the scientific facts mentioned in the Qur'ân were not known in that age, i.e., the Seventh Century CE. Having studied and examined the Arabic text of the Qur'ân, Dr. Bucaille says:

"I could not find a single error in the Qur'ân. I had to stop and ask myself: if a man was the author of the Qur'ân, how could he have written facts in the Seventh Century CE that today are shown to be in keeping with modern scientific knowledge? I had to acknowledge the evidence in front of me: the Qur'ân did not contain a single statement that was assailable from a modern scientific point of view. I repeated the same test for the Old Testament and the Gospels, always preserving the same objective outlook. In the former, I did not even have to go beyond the first book, Genesis, to find statements totally out of keeping with the cast-iron facts of modern science."[1]

Dr. Bucaille studied many scientific facts mentioned in the Qur'ân such as the creation of the universe, astronomy, the animal and botanical life, human reproduction and other related issues. I shall select, for the sake of brevity, two of the above issues to draw the attention of the reader to one of the objectives of this booklet.

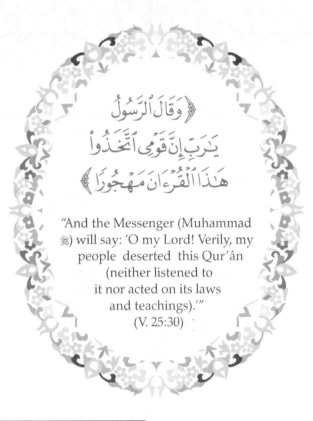

﴿ وَقَالَ ٱلرَّسُولُ
يَـٰرَبِّ إِنَّ قَوْمِى ٱتَّخَذُواْ
هَـٰذَا ٱلْقُرْءَانَ مَهْجُورًا ﴾

"And the Messenger (Muhammad
ﷺ) will say: 'O my Lord! Verily, my
people deserted this Qur'ân
(neither listened to
it nor acted on its laws
and teachings).'"
(V. 25:30)

---

[1]   The Bible, the Qur'ân and Science, p. 120

The Creation of the Heavens and the Earth

Man's knowledge of the origin of the universe is very limited. Scientists have proposed hypotheses and theories of evolution that are centered around one theme: the primordial fireball and the primordial era of matter and antimatter. According to the theories, the universe consisted mainly of strongly interacting particles. The primordial matter and antimatter, according to Encyclopaedia Britannica, eventually annihilated each other. Those particles that survived formed the present universe.[1] The basic process of the development of the universe is presented in the Qur'ân in simple words. Allâh ﷻ commands His Messenger

---

[1]	*Encyclopedia Britannica*, (15th ed.) Macropaedia, v. 18, p. 1008

Muhammad ﷺ to ask the disbelievers:

"Say (O Muhammad ﷺ): 'Do you verily disbelieve in Him Who created the earth in two Days? And you set up rivals (in worship) with Him? That is the Lord of the 'Alamîn (mankind, jinn and all that exists).' He placed therein (i.e. the earth) firm mountains from above it, and He blessed it, and measured therein its sustenance (for its dwellers) in four Days equal (i.e., all these four 'days' were equal in the length of time) for all those who ask (about its creation). Then He rose over (Istawâ) towards the heaven when it was smoke, and said to it and to the earth: 'Come both of you willingly or unwillingly.' They both said: 'We come willingly.' Then He completed and finished their creation (as) seven heavens in two Days and He made in each heaven its affair. And We adorned the nearest (lowest) heaven with lamps (stars)[1] to be an adornment as well as to guard (from the devils by using them as missiles against the devils). Such is the Decree of the All-Mighty, the All-Knower." (V. 41: 9-12)

And Allâh ﷻ says:

"Have not those who disbelieve known that the heavens and the earth were joined together as one united piece, then We parted them? And We have made from water every living thing. Will they not then believe?" (V. 21:30)

---

[1] (About the) Stars. Abu Qatâdah mentioned Allâh's Statement: "And We have adorned the nearest heaven with lamps," (V. 41:12) and said, "The creation of these stars is for three purposes, i.e., as decoration of the (nearest) heaven, as missiles to hit the devils, and as signs to guide travelers. So, if anybody tries to find a different interpretation, he is mistaken and just wastes his efforts, and troubles himself with what is beyond his limited knowledge." (Sahih Al-Bukhâri, The Book of the Beginning of Creation, Chap.3)

This concept of the division of one unit into two or more parts, and the celestial "smoke" referred to above, correspond to factual, scientific data. The Encyclopaedia Britannica wrote of the English physicist and astronomer, Sir James Jeans:

"We have found that, as Newton first conjectured a chaotic mass of gas of approximately uniform density and of very great extent, would be dynamically unstable: nuclei would tend to form in it, around which the whole of matter would ultimately condense." On the basis of this theory he proposed that all celestial objects originated by a process of fragmentation.[1]

Needless to say, the space program helped discover the homogeneity of the substances of which the moon, the earth, and other planets are formed. "Such statements in the Qur'ân concerning the creation, which appeared nearly fourteen centuries ago," Dr. Bucaille concluded, "obviously do not lend themselves to a human explanation."[2]

[1]   *Encyclopaedia Britannica* (15th ed.), Macropaedia, v. 18, p. 1009
[2]   Macropaedia, v. 18, p. 1008

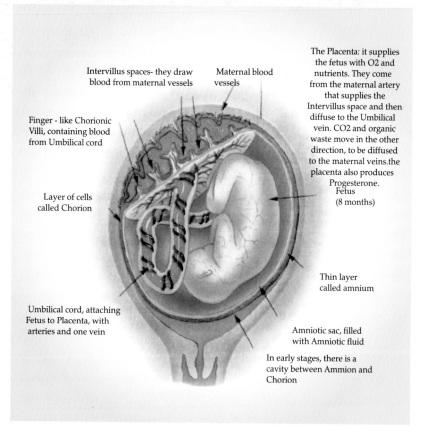

The Placenta: it supplies the fetus with O2 and nutrients. They come from the maternal artery that supplies the Intervillus space and then diffuse to the Umbilical vein. CO2 and organic waste move in the other direction, to be diffused to the maternal veins.the placenta also produces Progesterone.

Fetus (8 months)

Intervillus spaces- they draw blood from maternal vessels

Maternal blood vessels

Finger - like Chorionic Villi, containing blood from Umbilical cord

Layer of cells called Chorion

Umbilical cord, attaching Fetus to Placenta, with arteries and one vein

Thin layer called amnium

Amniotic sac, filled with Amniotic fluid

In early stages, there is a cavity between Ammion and Chorion

Complexities of human reproduction were decoded and understood only after the invention of the most sophisticated scientific and medical instruments, hundreds of years after the death of Prophet Muhammad ﷺ, yet the Qur'ân refers to the stages through which the human embryo passes.

As Allâh says:

"And indeed We created man (Adam) out of an extract of clay (water and earth). Thereafter We made him (the offspring of Adam) as a *Nutfah* (mixed drops of male and female sexual discharge and lodged it) in a safe lodging (womb of the woman). Then We made the *Nutfah* into a clot (a piece of thick coagulated blood), then We made the clot into a little lump of flesh, then We made out of that little lump of flesh bones, then We clothed the bones with flesh, and then We brought it forth as another creation. So, Blessed is Allâh, the Best of creators." (V. 23: 12-14)

Narrated 'Abdullâh ﷺ: Allâh's Messenger ﷺ, the true and truly inspired, said:

"(As regards your creation) every one of you is collected in the womb of his mother for the first forty days, and then he becomes a clot for another forty days, and then a piece of flesh for another forty days. Then Allâh sends an angel to write four words: He writes his deeds, time of his death, means of his livelihood, and whether he will be wretched or blessed (in the Hereafter). Then the soul is breathed into his body. So, a man may do deeds characteristic of the people of the (Hell) Fire, so much so that there is only the distance of a cubit between him and it, and then what has been written (by the angel) surpasses; and so he starts doing deeds characteristic of the people of Paradise and enters Paradise. Similarly, a person may do deeds characteristic of the people of Paradise, so much so that there is only the distance of a cubit between him and it, and then what has been written (by the angel) surpasses, and he starts doing deeds of the

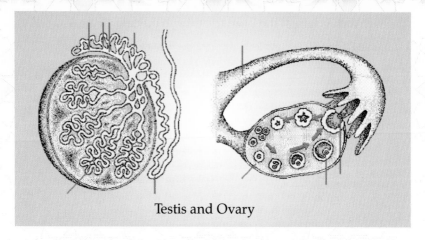
Testis and Ovary

people of the (Hell) Fire and enters the (Hell) Fire." [*Sahih Al-Bukhari, Hadith* No. 3332]

As scientifically proven, the stages of human reproduction are:

1. The fertilization of an ovum takes place in the Fallopian tubes. The fertilizing agent is the male sperm.

2. The implantation of the fertilized egg takes place at a precise spot in the female reproductive system. It descends into the uterus and lodges in the body of the uterus. As soon as the embryo is visible to the naked eye, it looks like a small mass of flesh. It grows there in progressive stages that are very well known today. They are the formations of the bone structure, the muscles, the nervous system, the circulation, and the viscera, etc.[1]

In conclusion, Dr. Bucaille ascertains:

"More than a thousand years before our time, at a period when attractive doctrines still prevailed, men had a knowledge of the Qur'ân. The statements it contains, express in simple terms, truths of earliest natural history which man has taken centuries to discover."[2]

---

[1] *Macropaedia*, v. 18, p. 1008
[2] *Bucaille*, op cit

Who is Muhammad?

Allâh ﷻ says in the Noble Qur'ân:

"And We have sent you (O Muhammad ﷺ) not but as a mercy for the 'Alamîn (mankind, jinn and all that exists). Say (O Muhammad ﷺ): 'It is revealed to me that your Ilâh (God) is only one Ilâh (God - Allâh). Will you then submit to His Will (become Muslims and stop worshiping others besides Allâh)?'" (V. 21: 107,108)

Muhammad ﷺ is the last of Allâh's Messengers and Prophets. His name is Muhammad, son of Abdullah. He was born in Makkah in 571 C.E. Prophet Muhammad ﷺ was, in his youth, a combination of the best social qualities. He was an exemplary man of weighty mind and faultless insight. He was favored with intelligence, originality of thought and accurate choice of the means to accurate goals. His long silence helped favorably in his habit of meditation and deep investigation into the truth. His vivid mind and pure nature were instrumental in assimilating and comprehending ways of life as well as individuals, groups and communities. He shunned superstitious practices but took an active part in useful and constructive activities. In the case of the useless and destructive dealings, he would have recourse to his self-adopted solitude. He refrained from drinking wine, eating meat slaughtered on stone altars or attending idolatrous festivals.

He proved himself to be the ideal of manhood, in possession of a spotless character. He was the most obliging to his compatriots, the most honest in his talk and the mildest in temper. He was the most gentle-hearted, chaste, and hospitable, and always impressed people by his piety-inspiring countenance. He was the most truthful and the best in keeping agreements. Due to the fine reputation he enjoyed among his people, they nicknamed him 'The Trustworthy.' There is a narration that highlights the different characteristics of the Prophet Muhammad ﷺ:

Narrated Ibn 'Abbâs رضى الله عنهما: Abu Sufyân narrated to me personally, saying,

"I set out during the truce that had been concluded between me and Allâh's Messenger ﷺ. While I was in Shâm, a letter sent by the Prophet ﷺ was brought to Heraclius. Dihya Al-Kalbi had brought and given it to the governor of Busra, and the latter forwarded it to Heraclius. Heraclius said, 'Is there anyone from the people of this man who claims to be a Prophet?' The people replied, 'Yes,' so, along with some other Quraishi men, I was called and we entered upon Heraclius, and we were seated in front of him. Then he said, 'Who amongst you is the nearest

relative to the man who claims to be a Prophet?' I (Abu Sufyân) replied: 'I am the nearest relative to him from amongst the group.' So they made me sit in front of him and made my companions sit behind me. Then he called upon his translator and said (to him). 'Tell them (i.e. Abu Sufyân's companions) that I am going to ask him (i.e. Abu Sufyân) regarding that man who claims to be a Prophet. So, if he tells me a lie, they should contradict him (instantly).' By Allâh, had I not been afraid that my companions would consider me a liar, I would have told lies. Heraclius then said to his translator, 'Ask him: What is his (i.e. the Prophet's) family status amongst you?' I said, 'He belongs to a noble family amongst us.' Heraclius said, 'Was any of his ancestors a king?' I said, 'No.' He said, 'Did you ever accuse him of telling lies before his saying what he has said?' I said, 'No.' He said, 'Do the nobles follow him or the poor people?' I said, 'It is the poor who follow him.' He said, 'Is the number of his followers increasing or decreasing?' I said, 'They are increasing.' He said, 'Does anyone renounce his religion (i.e. Islam) after embracing it, being displeased with it?' I said, 'No.' He said, 'Did you fight with him?' I replied, 'Yes.' He said, 'How was your fighting with him?' I said, 'The fighting between us was undecided and victory was shared by him and us in turns. He inflicts casualties upon us and we inflict casualties upon him.' He said, 'Did he ever betray?' I said, 'No, but now we are away from him in this truce and we do not know what he will do in it.'" Abu Sufyân added, "By Allâh, I was not able to insert in my speech a word (against him) except that. Heraclius said, 'Did anybody else (amongst you) ever claim the same (i.e. to be Allâh's Prophet) before him?' I said, 'No.' Then Heraclius told his translator to tell me (i.e. Abu Sufyân), 'I asked you about his family status amongst you, and you told me that he comes from a noble family amongst you. Verily, all Messengers come from the noblest family among their people. Then I asked you whether any of his ancestors was a king, and you denied that. Thereupon I thought that had one of his forefathers been a king, I would have said that he (i.e. Muhammad ﷺ) was seeking to rule the kingdom of his forefathers. Then I asked you regarding his followers, whether they were the noble or the poor among the people, and you said that they were only poor (who follow him). In fact, such are the followers of the Messengers. Then I asked you whether you have ever accused him of telling lies before he said what he said, and your reply was in the negative. Therefore, I took for granted that a man who did not tell a lie about others, could never tell a lie about Allâh. Then I asked you whether anyone of his followers had renounced his religion (i.e. Islam) after embracing it, being displeased with it, and you denied that. And such is Faith when its delight enters the heart and mixes with it completely. Then I asked you whether his followers were increasing or decreasing. You claimed that they were increasing, that is the way of true Faith till it is complete. Then I asked you whether you had ever fought with him, and you claimed that you had fought with him and the battle between you and him was undecided and the victory was shared by you and him in turns; he inflicted casualties upon you and you inflicted casualties upon them. Such is the case with the Messengers, they are put to trials and the final victory is for them. Then I asked you whether he has ever betrayed anyone; you claimed that he had never betrayed. Indeed, Messengers never betray. Then I asked you whether anyone had said this statement before him; and you denied that. Thereupon I thought if somebody had said that statement before him, then I would have said that he was but a man copying some sayings said before him.' Abu Sufyân said, "Heraclius then asked me, 'What does he order you to do?' I said, 'He orders us (to offer) prayers and (to pay) Zakât, and to keep good relationship with the kith and kin, and to be chaste.' Then Heraclius said, 'If whatever you have said is true, then he is really a Prophet. I knew that he (i.e. the Prophet ﷺ) was going to appear, but I never thought that he would be from amongst you. If I were certain that I can reach him, I would like to meet him and if I were with him, I would wash his feet; and his kingdom will expand (surely) to what is under my feet.' Then Heraclius asked for the letter of Allâh's Messenger ﷺ and read it, wherein was written:

In the Name of Allâh,
the Most Gracious, the Most Merciful.

(This letter is) from Muhammad, Messenger of Allâh, to Heraclius, the sovereign of Byzantine …Peace be upon him who follows the Right Path. Now then, I call you to embrace Islam. Embrace Islam and you will be saved (from Allâh's punishment); embrace Islam, and Allâh will give you a double reward, but if you reject this, you will be responsible for the sins of all the people of your kingdom: (Allâh's Statement:) "O people of the Scripture (Jews and Christians)! Come to a word that is just between us and you, that we worship none but Allâh (Alone) ... bear witness that we are Muslims." (V. 3: 64). "When he finished reading the letter, voices grew louder near him and there was a great hue and cry, and we were ordered to go out." Abu Sufyân added, "While coming out, I said to my companions, 'The matter of Ibn Abu Kabshah* (i.e. Muhammad ﷺ) has become so prominent that even the king of Banu Al-Asfar (i.e. the Romans) is afraid of him.' So I continued to believe that Allâh's Messenger ﷺ would be victorious, till Allâh made me embrace Islam. "Az-Zuhri said, "Heraclius then invited all the chiefs of the Byzantine and had them assembled in his house and said, 'O group of Byzantine! Do you wish to have a permanent success and guidance and that your kingdom should remain with you?' (Immediately after hearing that) they rushed towards the gate like angers, but they found them closed. Heraclius then said, 'Bring them back to me.' So he called them and said, 'I just wanted to test the strength of your adherence to your religion. Now I have observed of you that which I like.' Then the people fell in prostration before him and became pleased with him." (*Sahih Al-Bukhâri, Hadîth* No. 4553)

This impression on people can be deduced by the bliss that overwhelmed their hearts and filled them with dignity. Men's respect, awe and appreciation of Allâh's Messenger were unique and matchless. No other man in the whole world has been so honored and beloved. Those who knew him well were fascinated and enchanted by him. They were ready to sacrifice their lives for the sake of saving a nail of his from harm or injury. He had been favored with many aspects of perfection no one else had been granted, so his Companions found him peerless and loved him.

When he was blessed with the Prophethood at the age of forty, Allâh revealed the first Qur'ânic Verses to him through the angel Gabriel. He asked the Prophet ﷺ to preach the Oneness of Allâh and warn people against polytheism.

---

* Abu Kabshah was not the father of the Prophet ﷺ but it was a mockery done by Abu Sufyân out of hostility against the Prophet ﷺ.

> "Verily, We have sent the Revelation to you (O Muhammad ﷺ) as We sent the Revelation to Nûh (Noah) and the Prophets after him; We (also) sent the Revelation to Ibrâhîm (Abraham), Ismâ'îl (Ishmael), Ishâq (Isaac), Ya'qûb (Jacob), and Al-Asbât 'Isâ (Jesus), Ayub (Job), Yûnus (Jonah), Hârûn (Aaron), and Sulaimân (Solomon); and to Dâwûd (David) We gave the Zabûr (Psalms). And Messengers We have mentioned to you before, and Messengers We have not mentioned to you, – and to Mûsâ (Moses) Allâh spoke directly." (V.4: 163,164)

There is a narration that tells us how the Divine Revelations were revealed to the Prophet ﷺ:

Narrated 'Aishah رضى الله عنهما, the Mother of the faithful believers: Al-Hârith bin Hishâm asked Allâh's Messenger ﷺ: "O Allâh's Messenger! How is the Divine Revelation revealed to you?" Allâh's Messenger ﷺ replied, "Sometimes it is (revealed) like the ringing of a bell, this form of Revelation is the hardest of all and then this state passes off after I have grasped what is revealed. Sometimes the angel comes in the form of a man and talks to me and I grasp whatever he says. "'Aishah رضى الله عنهما added: "Verily, I saw the Prophet ﷺ being inspired divinely and noticed the sweat dropping from his forehead on a very cold day as the Revelation was over." (Sahih Al-Bukhâri, Hadîth No. 2)

The Mushrikeen of Makkah (polytheists and idolaters) opposed him and persecuted his followers severely, but that did not shake his faith nor cause his steadfastness to waiver. Nor did it stop more people from responding to his preaching. Finally, when the majority of the people of Al-Madinah embraced Islam, the Makkan Muslims migrated to Al-Madinah. Later on, Allâh's Messenger ﷺ too migrated to Al-Madinah to establish the Islamic State there. A few years later, the Mushrikeen of Makkah and their allies succumbed to the growing power of the Muslims, and Makkah was conquered without violence. Some thirty years after the death of the Prophet Muhammad ﷺ, Islam spread throughout the world, displacing the greatest two empires at the time, the Persian and the Roman.

> Narrated Abu Hurairah ؓ: Allâh's Messenger ﷺ said: "Both in this world and in the Hereafter, I am the nearest of all the people to 'Îsâ (Jesus) the son of Maryam (Mary). The Prophets are paternal brothers; their mothers are different, but their religion is one (i.e., Islamic Monotheism)." (Sahih Al-Bukhari, Hadith No. 3443)

Many Western scholars and famous personalities have admitted that no faults or flaws are to be found in the character and behavior of the Prophet ﷺ. Some of their observations are remarkable. George Bernard Shaw wrote:

"I believe that if a man like him were to assume the dictatorship of the modern world, he would succeed in solving the problems in a way that would bring the much needed peace and happiness."

Lamartine praised the Prophet ﷺ writing:

"If greatness of purpose, smallness of means and astounding results are the three criteria of human genius, who could claim to compare any great man in modern history with Muhammad?"[1]

The Hindu leader Mahatma Gandhi wrote about the Prophet ﷺ:

"I become more than ever convinced that it was not the sword that won a place for Islam in those days. It was the rigid simplicity, the utter self-effacement of the Prophet, the scrupulous regard for pledges, his intense devotion to his friends and followers and his intrepidity, his fearlessness, his absolute trust in God and in his own mission. These and not the sword carried everything before them and surmounted every obstacle."[2]

---

[1] *Histoire de la Turquie*, 1855.   [2] *Young India*, 1992.

What is Islam?

Islam is the last of all the Divine faiths. Its name was instituted by the Qur'ân during the Farewell Pilgrimage:

"This day, I have perfected your religion for you, completed My Favor upon you, and have chosen for you Islam as your religion." (V. 5:3)

Islam is the last of the universal faiths. Today it numbers over 1.25 billion followers. Every country in the world has at least a small Muslim minority. Islam has shown itself to be not only the most widespread faith in the world, but also the most dynamic one, attracting converts at a faster rate than at any time in the last few centuries.

The Arabic term 'Islam', meaning 'submission', points to a fundamental religious tenet that a Muslim submits to the Will of Allâh ﷻ by conforming inwardly and outwardly to His law. Islam is not a "religion" in the narrow sense used by secular humanists in the West, but it is the universal and eternal religion made known through Prophets to every nation or people since the human race first began. This religion of Islam lays great emphasis on uncompromising monotheism and strict adherence to its creed and its method of worship. It enjoins submission to the Will of Allâh ﷻ and urges every person to follow as closely as possible the exemplary way of the life of Muhammad ﷺ, the last of the Prophets and Messengers.

وَمَا خَلَقْتُ الْجِنَّ وَالْإِنسَ إِلَّا لِيَعْبُدُونِ ﴿٥٦﴾

"And I (Allâh) created not the jinn and mankind except that they should worship Me (Alone)." (V. 51:56)

Allâh ﷻ created the universe and what is in it so that He would be recognized as the One and only God. He created men and jinn only to celebrate His praise, and worship Him. Allâh ﷻ says:

The method and form of worship are not left to man's whim or discretion. Allâh ﷻ is the One Who ordains and decrees all acts of worship and how they must be performed. Since Islam deals with every aspect of life, spiritual and physical, its jurisprudence is based on Islamic Faith (Belief) worship, admonitions and ordinances dealing with social, economic and political transactions.

Because Islam is a perfect way of life, it enjoins the maintenance of a refined standard of character. Allâh's Messenger ﷺ said:

"Verily, I have been sent to perfect the refined behavior."

Allâh ﷻ praised the model behavior of His Messenger ﷺ by saying:

﴿ وَإِنَّكَ لَعَلَىٰ خُلُقٍ عَظِيمٍ ﴾

"And verily, you (O Muhammad ﷺ) are on an exalted (standard of) character." (V. 68:4)

'Âishah رضى الله عنهما, the wife of Allâh's Messenger ﷺ, was asked about his behavior. She said: "His standard of behavior was the Qur'ân." 'Aishah رضى الله عنهما meant that the Prophet ﷺ adhered strictly to the Qur'ân, to its rules of discipline, commands, and prohibitions and to all its excellent, beautiful, and gracious teachings. For this reason, Allâh ﷻ commands the believers to follow the exemplary life of His Messenger ﷺ: "Indeed in the Messenger of Allâh (Muhammad ﷺ) you have a good example to follow." (V. 33:21)

Islam enjoins good character expressed in good manners for every occasion, e.g., on greeting, sitting, eating, learning, teaching, sporting, traveling, dressing, visiting, sleeping, treating people, particularly relatives and neighbors with kindness, etc. Codes for all such aspects of refined behavior are found in both the Qur'ân and the traditions of Allâh's Messenger ﷺ.

The family enjoys a high status in Islam. It is the core of the society, because a healthy family means a healthy society. Hence Allâh ﷻ commands that parents be treated with gentleness and submissiveness saying:

"And your Lord has decreed that you worship none but Him. And that you be dutiful to your parents. If one of them or both of them attain old age in your life, say not to them a word of disrespect, nor shout at them but address them in terms of honor. And lower to them the wing of submission and humility through mercy, and say: 'My Lord! Bestow on them Your Mercy as they did bring me up when I was young.'" (V. 17:23, 24)

Next to the immediate family come kinfolk. Allâh's Messenger ﷺ said that Allâh ﷻ has promised to be kind to the person who treats his kin with kindness, and to bar from Allâh's Mercy the person who severs relations with his relatives.

The Pillars of Islam

THE HAJJ | THE ZAKÂT | TWO TESTIMONIES | THE PRAYER | THE FAST

The Levels of Faith

'Umar bin Al-Khattab ⚅ reported:

One day while we were sitting with Allâh's Messenger ⚅, a man with black hair came in wearing white clothes. He showed no sign of travel. Nor could any of us recognize him. He sat facing the Prophet ⚅ with his knees touching the Prophet's knees. He placed his hands on the thighs of the Prophet ⚅ and said, "Muhammad! Tell me what Islam is?" The Prophet ⚅ said, "Islam is testifying that none has the right to be worshipped but Allâh, and that Muhammad is the Messenger of Allâh, performing the prayers (Iqâmat-as-Salât), paying the poor due or obligatory charity (Zakât), observing the fast (*Saum*) of the month of Ramadân, and performing the pilgrimage (*Hajj*), if you can afford it." The man said, "You have told the truth." ['Umar ﷺ said, "We were amazed that first he asked him and then himself approved of his answer."] The man further asked, "Tell me, what is Belief?" The Prophet ﷺ said, "It is to believe in Allâh, and His Angels, His Books, His Messengers, and to believe in the Last Day and in the Divine Preordainment (*Qadâ'*) and its good and evil consequences." "You have told the truth," he said. Then he asked, "Tell me, what is Perfection (*Ihsân*)?" He said, "It is to worship Allâh as though you see Him. Although you do not see Him, He sees you." He said, "Tell me, when is the Final Hour?" The Prophet ﷺ said, "The one who is asked has no more knowledge about it than the one who is asking." He said, "Tell me then about its signs." The Prophet ﷺ said, "When a female slave gives birth to her own mistress, and when you see the poor naked shepherds compete with one another in erecting tall buildings." Then the man left. The Prophet ﷺ kept thinking for a while and then asked me, "'Umar, do you know who was the questioner?" I said, "Allâh and His Messenger know best." He said, "That was Gabriel. He came to teach you people your religion." (*Al-Bukhâri* and *Sahih Muslim*)

Allâh's Messenger ﷺ said that Islam is built on five pillars:

1. *Shahadah* Confession of a Muslim (*Lâ ilâha illallâh Muhammad-ur-Rasûl-Allâh* None has the right to be worshipped but Allâh and Muhammad ﷺ is the Messenger of Allâh)
2. *Salât* (*Iqamat-as-Salat*) (Prayer)
3. To pay the *Zakât* (The poor due or obligatory charity)
4. *Saum* (Fasting) (to fast in the month of Ramadan)
5. *Hajj* (The Pilgrimage) to Makkah

Shahadah – Confession of a Muslim

لا إلـــــه إلا الله مـــحــمـــد رســـول الله

Lâ ilâha illallâh, Muhammad-ur-Rasûl-Allâh

(None has the right to be worshipped but Allâh, and
Muhammad (ﷺ) is the Messenger of Allâh).

We have noticed that most of mankind, who embrace Islam, do
not understand the reality of the meaning of the first fundamental
principle of Islam, i.e. *Lâ ilâha illallâh, Muhammad-ur-Rasûl-Allâh*
(none has the right to be worshipped but Allâh, and Muhammad
is the Messenger of Allâh). So, we consider it essential to explain
something of the meanings of this great principle in some detail:

لا إلـــــه إلا الله مـــحــمـــد رســـول الله

Lâ ilâha illallâh, Muhammad-ur- Rasûl-Allâh

"None has the right to be worshipped but Allâh and
Muhammad ﷺ is the Messenger of Allâh", has three aspects:
A, B and C.

A. It is that, you have to pledge a covenant with (Allâh), the Creator of the heavens and earth, the Ruler of all that exists, the Lord of Majesty and Highness, on four points (or conditions):

Point I: A confession with your heart that the Creator (of everything) is Allâh; it is that you have to say: "I testify that the Creator of all the universe including the stars, the planets, the sun, the moon, the heavens, the earth with all its known and unknown forms of life, is Allâh. He is the Organizer and Planner of all its affairs. It is He Who gives life and death, and He (i.e. Allâh Alone) is the Sustainer, and the Giver of security." And this is called (your confession for the) "Oneness of the Lordship of Allâh," – *Tauhid-ar-Rubûbiyyah.*

Point II: A confession with your heart that: "I testify that none has the right to be worshipped but Allâh Alone." The word "Worship" (i.e. *'Ibâdah*) carries a great number of meanings in the Islamic terminology: it conveys that all kinds of worship are meant for Allâh Alone and none else, whether it be an angel, Messenger, Prophet 'Îsâ (Jesus) – son of Maryam (Mary), 'Uzair (Ezra), Muhammad, saint, idol, the sun, the moon and all other kinds of false deities. So pray to none but Allâh, invoke none but Allâh, ask for help from none (unseen) but Allâh, swear by none but Allâh, offer an animal as sacrifice to none but Allâh,... etc, and that means, – all that Allâh and

﴿ فَٱعۡلَمۡ أَنَّهُۥ لَآ إِلَٰهَ إِلَّا ٱللَّهُ وَٱسۡتَغۡفِرۡ لِذَنۢبِكَ وَلِلۡمُؤۡمِنِينَ وَٱلۡمُؤۡمِنَٰتِۗ وَٱللَّهُ يَعۡلَمُ مُتَقَلَّبَكُمۡ وَمَثۡوَىٰكُمۡ ﴾

"So know (O Muhammad ﷺ) that, *Lâ ilâha illallâh* (none has the right to be worshipped but Allâh), and ask forgiveness for your sin, and also for (the sin of) believing men and believing women. And Allâh knows well your moving about, and your place of rest (in your homes)." (V.47:19)

His Messenger Muhammad ﷺ order you to do, (in the Qur'ân and in the *Sunnah* (legal ways of Prophet Muhammad ﷺ) you must do, and all that Allâh and His Messenger Muhammad ﷺ forbid you, you must not do. And this is called (your confession for the) "Oneness of the worship of Allâh," *Tauhid-al-Ulûhiyyah*. And that you (mankind) worship none but Allâh.

Point III: A confession with your heart that: "O Allâh! I testify that all the best of names and the most perfect qualities with which You have named or qualified Yourself in Your Book (i.e. the Qur'ân) or as Your Prophet Muhammad ﷺ has named or qualified You with his statement, I believe that all those (names and qualities) are for You without changing their meanings or neglecting them completely or likening them (giving resemblance) to others." As Allâh says:

"There is nothing like Him, and He is the All-Hearer, the All-Seer." (V. 42:11)

This Noble Verse confirms the quality of hearing and the quality of sight for Allâh without likening them (giving resemblance) to others, and He also says:

"To one whom I have created with Both My Hands," (V. 38:75)

and He also says:

"The Hand of Allâh is over their hands." (V. 48:10)

This confirms two Hands for Allâh, but there is no similarity for them. Similarly Allâh ﷻ says:

"The Most Gracious (Allâh) rose over (*Istawa*) the (Mighty) Throne." (V. 20:5)

"Muhammad is the Messenger of Allâh. And those who are with him are severe against disbelievers, and merciful among themselves..." (V. 48:29)

So He rose over the Throne really in a manner that suits His Majesty. And Allâh is over His Throne over the seventh heaven, as the slave-girl pointed towards the heavens, when Allâh's Messenger (Muhammad ﷺ) asked her as to where Allâh is. He only comes down over the first (nearest) heaven to us during the last third part of every night and also on the day of 'Arafah (Hajj, i.e. the 9th of Dhul-Hijjah), as mentioned by the Prophet ﷺ, but He is with us by His Knowledge only, not by His Personal-Self (Bi-Dhâtihi). It is not as some people say that Allâh is present everywhere – here, there, and even inside the breasts of men. He sees and hears all that we do or utter. And this is called (your confession for the) "Oneness of the Names and Qualities of Allâh" Tauhîd-al-Asmâ was-Sifât and this is the right Belief, the Belief which was followed by the Messengers of Allâh [from Nûh (Noah), Ibrâhîm (Abraham), Mûsa (Moses), Dâwûd (David), Sulaimân (Solomon), 'Îsâ (Jesus) to Muhammad عليهم الصلاة والسلام and the Companions of Prophet Muhammad ﷺ and the righteous followers of these Messengers عليهم السلام

Point IV: A confession with your heart: "O Allâh! I testify that Muhammad ﷺ is Your Messenger." That means that none has the right to be followed after Allâh, but Prophet Muhammad ﷺ as he is the last of His Messengers. As Allâh says:

"Muhammad (ﷺ) is not the father of any of your men, but he is the Messenger of Allâh and the last (end) of the Prophets. And Allâh is Ever All-Aware of everything." (V. 33:40)

"And whatsoever the Messenger (Muhammad ﷺ) gives you, take it; and whatsoever he forbids you, abstain (from it)." (V. 59:7)

And Allâh says:

"Say (O Muhammad ﷺ to mankind): 'If you (really) love Allâh then follow me (i.e. accept Islamic Monotheism, follow the Qur ân and the Sunnah).'" (V. 3:31)

As for others than Muhammad ﷺ, their statements are to be taken or rejected as to whether these are in accordance with

((يَاأَيُّهَا النَّاسُ : قُولُوا لَا إِلٰه إِلا اللهِ، تُفلِحُوا)) (احمد)

> Narrated Rabee'h bin Ubaid ﴾: "The Prophet ﷺ said: 'O people: Pronounce *Lâ ilâha illallâh*, you will be successful.'" (*Ahmad*)

Allâh's Book (i.e. The Qur'ân) and with the *Sunnah* (legal ways, orders, acts of worship, statements) of the Prophet ﷺ or not. As the Divine Revelation has stopped after the death of Prophet Muhammad ﷺ and it will not resume except at the time of the Descent of 'Îsâ (Jesus) – son of Maryam (Mary) and he (i.e. Jesus) will rule with justice according to the Islamic laws, during the last days of the world as it has been mentioned in the authentic *Hadîth* (i.e. narration of Prophet Muhammad ﷺ). (*Sahih-Al-Bukhari*, *Hadîth* No. 2222)

B. It is essential to utter: *Lâ ilâha illallâh, Muhammad-ur-Rasûl Allâh* (none has the right to be worshipped but Allâh, and Muhammad is the Messenger of Allâh.) As it has come in the statement of Prophet Muhammad ﷺ to his uncle Abû Tâlib at the time of the latter's death: "O uncle, if you utter it (*Lâ ilâh illallâh, Muhammad-ur-Rasûl Allâh,* none has the right to be worshipped but Allâh, and Muhammad ﷺ is the Messenger of Allâh), then I shall be able to argue on your behalf before Allâh, on the Day of Resurrection." Similarly, when Abû Dharr Al-Ghifârî embraced Islam, he went to *Al-Masjid-al-Harâm* and he proclaimed it loudly in front of the Quraish infidels until he was beaten severely.

C. It is essential that the limbs and all the other parts and organs of one's body testify to it, and this is very important as regards its meaning (i.e., the meaning of *Lâ ilâha illallâh Muhammad-ur-Rasul Allâh* none has the right to be worshipped but Allâh, and Muhammad ﷺ is the Messenger of Allâh). So whoever has confessed this (to his Lord), he shall not commit sins like robbing, killing, stealing, illegal sexual intercourse, eating pig meat, drinking alcoholic beverages, taking undue advantage of orphan's property, cheating in trade, bribery and earning money through illegal means, telling lies, backbiting etc., or otherwise the limbs and all the other parts and organs of his body will testify against him that he was a liar in his words which he pledged to Allâh. In case he commits the above sins, he should know that it is a sin that obliges him to repent to Allâh, and ask His forgiveness, as (his) body parts (i.e. skin, private parts, hands, tongue, ears, etc.) will testify to the above mentioned crimes (i.e. actions) against himself on the Day of Resurrection.

And with the confession of this great sentence (i.e. principle) a person enters in the fold of the Islamic religion accordingly, it is essential for him to believe in all the Messengers of Allâh and not to differentiate between them. As it is mentioned in His Book, Allâh says:

"Do then those who disbelieve think that they can take My slaves [i.e. the angels; Allâh's Messengers; 'Îsâ (Jesus), son of Maryam (Mary)] as *Auliyâ'* (lords, gods, protectors) besides Me? Verily, We have prepared Hell as an entertainment for the disbelievers (in the Oneness of Allâh – Islamic Monotheism). "Say (O Muhammad ﷺ): 'Shall We tell you about the greatest losers in respect of (their) deeds?' Those whose efforts have been wasted in this life while they thought they were acquiring good by their deeds! They are those who deny the *Ayât* (proofs, evidences, verses, lessons, signs, revelations, etc.) of their Lord and the Meeting with Him (in the Hereafter). So their works are in vain, and on the Day of Resurrection, We shall assign no weight for them. That shall be their recompense, Hell; because they disbelieved and took My *Ayât* (proofs, evidences, verses, lessons, revelations, etc.) and My Messengers by way of jest and mockery. Verily! Those who believe (in the Oneness of Allâh – Islamic Monotheism) and do righteous deeds, shall have the Gardens of *Al-Firdaus* (Paradise) for their entertainment. Wherein they shall dwell (forever). No desire will they have to be removal therefrom. Say (O Muhammad ﷺ to mankind): 'If the sea were ink for (writing) the Words of my Lord, surely the sea would be exhausted before the Words of my Lord would be finished even if we brought (another sea) like it for its aid.' Say (O Muhammad ﷺ): 'I am only a man like you, it has been revealed to me that your *Ilâh* (God) is One *Ilâh* (God, – i.e. Allâh). So whoever hopes for the Meeting with his Lord, let him work righteousness and associate none as a partner in the worship of his Lord." (V. 18:102-110)

This introduction is necessary for anyone who wishes to embrace Islam. After this confession he (or she) should take a bath (i.e. *Ghusl*) and then offer a two *Rak'at* prayer, and act upon the five principles of Islam, as narrated by Ibn 'Umar رضي الله عنهما in the Book, *Sahih Al-Bukhari, Hadîth* No. 8:

Narrated Ibn 'Umar رضي الله عنهما: Allâh's Messenger ﷺ said: Islam is based on the following five (principles):

1. To testify *Lâ ilâha illallâh wa anna Muhammad-ur-Rasul-Allâh* (none has the right to be worshipped but Allâh and that Muhammad is the Messenger of Allâh).
2. To perform *Salât* (*Iqâmat As-Salât*).
3. To pay *Zakât*. (Obligatory Charity)
4. To perform *Hajj* (i.e. pilgrimage to Makkah).
5. To observe *Saum* (fast) during the month of Ramadân.

And must believe in the six articles of Faith, i.e. to believe in:

(1) Allâh, (2) His angels, (3) His Messengers, (4) His revealed Books, (5) the Day of Resurrection, and (6) *Al-Qadar* (Divine Preordainments i.e. Whatever Allâh has ordained must come to pass).

Salât (Prayer)

The Arabic word *Salât* linguistically means supplication, but ritually, is the performance of a set and regular physical routine positions with the recitation of Verses from the Qur'ân and certain appropriate supplications.

The recitation of *Sûrat Al-Fâtihah* in each *Rak'at* is compulsory:

"In the Name of Allâh, the Most Gracious, the Most Merciful. All praise and thanks are Allâh's, the Lord of the *'Alamîn* (mankind, jinn and all that exists). The Most Gracious, the Most Merciful. The Only Owner (and the Only Ruling Judge) of the Day of Recompense (i.e. the Day of Resurrection). You (Alone) we worship, and You (Alone) we ask for help (for each and everything). Guide us to the Straight Way. The way of those on whom You have bestowed Your Grace, not (the way) of those who earned Your Anger,[1] nor of those who went astray." (V. 1: 1-7)

It is a means of communication between man and Allâh. In it, a person demonstrates his love and submissiveness to Allâh. It is called the pillar on which Islam stands. It is an act of worship which combines the positions of standing, bowing, prostrating and sitting with such utterances as the *Takbîr*, the saying of *Allâhu*

---

[1] Narrated Adi bin Hâtim ؓ: "I asked Allâh's Messenger ﷺ about the Statement of Allâh: 1." غير المغضوب عليهم *Ghairil maghdubi 'alaihim* [not (the way) of those who earned Your Anger]," he replied: "They are the Jews." And 2. " والضالين *Walad dâllîn* (nor of those who went astray)," he replied: "The Christians, and they are the ones who went astray." [This *Hadith* is quoted by At-Tirmidhi and Abu Dâwûd]

Narrated Ibn 'Umar رضى الله عنهما: Zaid bin 'Amr bin Nufail went to Shâm (the region comprising Syria, Lebanon, Palestine and Jordan), enquiring about a true religion to follow. He met a Jewish religious scholar and asked him about their religion. He said, "I intend to embrace your religion, so tell me something about it." The Jew said, "You will not embrace our religion unless you receive your share of Allâh's Anger." Zaid said, "I do not run except from Allâh's Anger, and I will never bear a bit of it if I have the power to avoid it. Can you tell me of some other religion?" He said, "I do not know any other religion except *Hanîf* (Islamic Monotheism)." Zaid enquired, "What is *Hanîf*?" He said, "*Hanîf* is the religion of (the Prophet) Abraham (عليه السلام), he was neither a Jew nor a Christian, and he used to worship none but Allâh [(Alone) Islâmic Monotheism]." Then Zaid went out and met a Christian religious scholar and told him the same (as before). The Christian said, "You will not embrace our religion unless you get a share of Allâh's Curse." Zaid replied, "I do not run except from Allâh's Curse, and I will never bear any of Allâh's Curse and His Anger if I have the power to avoid them. Will you tell me of some other religion?" He replied, "I do not know any other religion except *Hanîf* (Islamic Monotheism)." Zaid enquired, "What is *Hanîf*?" He replied "*Hanîf* is the religion of (the Prophet) Abraham (عليه السلام) he was neither a Jew nor a Christian, (and he used to worship none but Allâh [(Alone) Islâmic Monotheism]." When Zaid heard their statement about (the religion of) Abraham, he left that place, and when he came out, he raised both his hands and said, "O Allâh! I make You my Witness that I am on the religion of Abraham." (*Sahih Al-Bukhâri, Hadîth* No. 3827)

Akbar (Allâh is the Most Great!); the *Taslîm*, the saying of *As-salâmu 'alaikum wa rahmatullâhi wa barakâtuhu* (May the Peace, Mercy and Blessings of Allâh be upon you!).

It is considered as the light of the believer, a protection against the commission of sins and a means of atonement for past sins.

The Importance of *Salât*

Salât (prayer) is obligatory on every adult Muslim, and children should be taught how to perform the prayers. The delay of prayers beyond their fixed time without a valid or legitimate reason is prohibited. The Prophet ﷺ said:

> "Any Muslim who performs an obligatory prayer after having done its ablution (*Wudû'* in Arabic, i.e., the ritual washing of certain parts of the body), bowing and prostration, will have his previous sins erased as long as he keeps away from committing major sins. This applies throughout one's lifetime." [1]

Denial of *Salât* (prayers) as an obligatory act of worship constitutes apostasy from Islam, while neglecting it is an act of infidelity. *Salât* was ordained obligatory when the Prophet ﷺ was conveyed to the seventh heaven on a miraculous trip.

It will be the first thing about which man is questioned on the Day of Resurrection.

Not only is *Salât* obligatory, it must also be performed at five prescribed times every day. The following are the five daily prayers:

1. The Dawn Prayer (*Salâtul-Fajr*): It consists of two obligatory

---

[1] Each individual will be held accountable for every minute thing he does, and shall stand all by himself on the Day of Reckoning to be questioned by Allâh. Everyone is responsible for his own deeds. One's life in the Hereafter is either everlasting happiness or everlasting torment.

units (two *Rak'ât* in Arabic). Two optional units of prayer (*Sunnah*) precede the Dawn Prayer. The period of this prayer is from the crack of dawn to sunrise.

2. The Noon Prayer (*Salâtuz-Zuhr*): It is comprised of four obligatory units. It is preceded by four optional units (in two groups of two) and followed by two optional units. It is performed after the sun passes its zenith until the second half of the afternoon, '*Asr* in Arabic.

3. The Afternoon Prayer (*Salâtul-'Asr*): This prayer is four obligatory units and is performed when the length of the shadow of a vertical stick equals the length of the stick. The prayer period lasts until just before sunset. One may perform four optional units before the obligatory units.

4. The Evening Prayer (*Salâtul-Maghrib*): It consists of three obligatory units, followed by two optional ones. The Evening Prayer may be performed soon as the sun sinks below the horizon until dusk has ended.

5. The Night Prayer (*Salâtul-'Ishâ'*): This last of the five daily prayers consists of four obligatory units. It may be preceded by two optional units and followed by two, then three or one (*Witr*) optional units. It is performed after it has become completely dark until the crack of dawn, but it is preferable to perform it before midnight.

The performing of *As-Salât* (the prayers) means:

(A) Each and every Muslim, male or female, is obliged to offer his *Salât* (prayers) regularly five times a day at the specified times; the male in the mosque in congregation and as for the female, it is better to offer them at home. As the Prophet has said:

"Order your children to offer *Salât* (prayers) at the age of seven and beat them (about it) at the age of ten."

The chief (of a family, town, tribe, etc.) and the Muslim ruler of a country are held responsible before Allâh in case of non-fulfillment of this obligation by the Muslims under his authority.

(B) To perform the *Salât* (prayers) in a way just as Prophet Muhammad ﷺ used to perform it with all its rules and regulations, i.e. standing, bowing, prostrating it." (*Sahih Al-Bukhâri*) the *Salât* (prayer) begins with *Takbîr* (*Allâhu-Akbar*) with the recitation of *Sûrat Al-Fâtihah* etc. along with its various postures, standing, bowing, prostrations, sitting etc. and it ends with *Taslîm*.

To perform prayer, one must be in the state of ritual purity obtained after an ablution (*Wudû'*). The ablution includes washing the hands, rinsing the nose and the mouth, washing the face and the arms, wiping the head with wet hands and washing the feet, as Allâh says:

"O you who believe! When you intend to offer *As-Salât* (the prayer), wash your faces and your hands (forearms) up to the elbows, rub (by passing wet hands over) your heads, and (wash) your feet up to the ankles.[1] If you are in a state of *Janâba* (i.e. after a sexual discharge), purify yourselves (bathe your whole body). But if you are ill or on a journey, or any of you comes from the *Ghâ'it* (toilet), or you have been in contact with women (i.e. sexual intercourse), and

---

[1] The superiority of ablution. And *Al-Ghurr-ul-Muhajjalûn* the parts of the body of the Muslims washed in ablution will shine on the Day of Resurrection and the angels will call them by that name) from the traces of ablution.

Narrated Nu'aim Al-Mujmir: Once I went up the roof of the mosque along with Abu Hurairah ﷺ. He performed ablution and said, " I heard the Prophet ﷺ saying, 'On the Day of Resurrection, my followers will be called *Al-Ghurr-ul-Muhajjalun* from the traces of ablution and whoever can increase the area of his radiance* should do so (by performing ablution in the most perfect manner).'" (*Sahih Al-Bukhâri, Hadîth* No.136).

* The Prophet ﷺ did not increase the area more than what is washed of the body parts while doing ablution as Allâh ordered to be washed in the Qur'ân. [For details about *Wudû'* (ablution), see *Sahih Al-Bukhâri*, (The Book of Ablution)].

you find no water, then perform *Tayammum* with clean earth and rub therewith your faces and hands.[1] Allâh does not want to place you in difficulty, but He wants to purify you, and to complete His Favour to you that you may be thankful." (V. 5:6)

Prayer is the pillar of Islam. It is the first act of worship for which man is answerable on the Day of Reckoning. If Allâh accepts one's prayer, then He accepts the rest of his good deeds as well.

The sin of one who misses the 'Asr prayer (intentionally)

Narrated Ibn 'Umar   that Allâh's Messenger said:

"Whoever misses the *'Asr* prayer (intentionally), then it is as if he lost his family and property." (*Sahih Al-Bukhâri, Hadîth* No. 557)

Narrated Jâbir bin 'Abdullâh رضى الله عنهما I heard Allâh's Messenger saying, "Verily, between a man (i.e., a Muslim, believer of Islamic Monotheism) and between *Shirk* (polytheism) and *Kufr* (disbelief) is the abandoning of As-*Salât* (prayer)." [*Sahih Muslim, Hadith* No. 146]

One who omits (does not offer) the 'Asr prayer (intentionally)

The one who omits (does not offer) the 'Asr prayer intentionally until its stated time is over and if he prays after that time, then it is useless.

Narrated Abul-Malîh: We were with Buraidah in a battle on a cloudy day and he said, "Offer the 'Asr prayer early as the Prophet said, 'Whoever omits the 'Asr prayer, all his (good) deeds will be lost.'" (*Sahih Al-Bukhâri, Hadîth* No. 528)

---

[1] Strike your hands on the earth and then pass the palm of each on the back of the other and then blow off the dust from them and then pass (rub) them on your face: this is called *Tayammum*.

Zakât (the Poor Due or Obligatory Charity)

Zakât is due on all types of properties to be given out to the poor Muslims as stated in the following Qur'ânic instructions:

"*As-Sadaqât* (here it means *Zakât*) are only for the *Fuqarâ'* (poor), and *Al-Masâkin*[1] (the needy) and those employed to collect (the funds); and to attract the hearts of those who have been inclined (towards Islam), and to free the captives; and for those in debt, and for Allâh's cause (i.e. for *Mujahidûn* – those fighting in a holy battle), and for the wayfarer (a traveller who is cut off from everything); a duty imposed by Allâh. And Allâh is All-Knower, All-Wise." (V. 9:60)

---

[1]   Narrated Abu Hurairah ﷺ: Allâh's Messenger ﷺ said, "*Al-Miskîn* (the poor) is not the one who goes round the people and asks them for a mouthful or two (of meals) or a date or two, but *Al-Miskîn* (the poor) is that who has not enough (money) to satisfy his needs and whose condition is not known to others, that others may give him something in charity, and who does not beg of people." (*Sahih Al-Bukhâri, Hadith* No. 1479)

Zakât purifies the donor from stinginess, miserliness and greed. It also signifies the social welfare system that fosters brotherly love, friendship and cooperation among Muslims. It further bridges the gap between the rich and the poor on a basis of mercy and kindness. Moreover, Allâh rewards it generously.

The Prophet ﷺ said:

"He who pays *Zakât*, wards off the evil of his property."

Zakât is due on the properties of all Muslims, be they old or young, male or female, sane or insane. It is due on the following properties:

1. Gold, silver and money
2. Livestock
3. Produce
4. Commercial commodities and stocks
5. Treasures and mines

If a person dies before paying the *Zakât* due on his or her property, then it must be taken from the estate of the deceased before its division among the heirs.

Allâh the Exalted has promised severe torment for those who withhold *Zakât*.

He said:

"And let not those who covetously withhold of that which Allâh has bestowed on them of His bounty (Wealth) think that it is good for them (and so they do not pay the obligatory *Zakât*). Nay, it will be worse for them; the things which they covetously withheld, shall be tied to their necks like a collar on the Day of Resurrection. And to Allâh belongs the heritage of the heavens and the earth; and Allâh is Well-Acquainted with all that you do." (V. 3:180)

Narrated Abu Hurairah ؓ that Allah's Messenger ﷺ said:

"Anyone whom Allah has given wealth but he does not pay its *Zakât*; then, on the Day of Resurrection, his wealth will be presented to him in the shape of a bald-headed poisonous male snake with two poisonous glands in its mouth and it will encircle itself round his neck and bite him over his cheeks and say, 'I am your wealth; I am your treasure.'" Then the Prophet ﷺ recited this Divine Verse: "And let not those who covetously withhold of that which Allah has bestowed on them of His bounty." (V. 3:180) (*Sahih Al-Bukhâri, Hadith* No. 4565)

There is another *Hadith* narrated by Abu Hurairah ﷺ:

When the Prophet ﷺ died and Abu Bakr became his successor and some of the Arabs reverted to disbelief, 'Umar said: "O Abu Bakr! How can you fight these people although Allâh's Messenger ﷺ said, 'I have been ordered to fight the people till they say: *Lâ ilâha illallâh* (none has the right to be worshiped but Allâh), and whoever said *Lâ ilâha illallâh*, Allâh will save his property and his life from me, unless (he does something for which he receives legal punishment) justly, and his account will be with Allâh?' Abu Bakr said, 'By Allâh! I will fight whoever differentiates between *Salât* (prayers) and *Zakât* (obligatory charity); as *Zakât* is the right to be taken from property (according to Allâh's Orders). By Allâh! If they refused to pay me even a kid they used to pay to Allâh's Messenger , I would fight with them for withholding it.' 'Umar said, 'By Allâh! It was nothing, but I noticed that Allâh opened Abu Bakr's chest towards the decision to fight, therefore I realized that his decision was right.'" (*Sahih Al-Bukhâri, Hadith* No. 6924, 6925)

The Prophet ﷺ also said:

"(On the Day of Resurrection) camels will come to their owners in the best state of health they have ever had (in the world), and if he had not paid their *Zakât* (in the world) then they would tread him with their feet; and similarly, sheep will come to their owners in the best state of health they have ever had in the world, and if he had not paid their *Zakât*, then they would tread him with their hooves and would butt him with their horns." The Prophet ﷺ added, 'One of their rights is that they should be milked while water is kept in front of them.' The Prophet ﷺ added, 'I do not want anyone of you to come to me on the Day of Resurrection, carrying over his neck a sheep that will be bleating.' Such a person will (then) say, 'O Muhammad! (please intercede for me).' I will say to him, 'I can't help you, for I conveyed Allâh's Message to you.' Similarly, I do not want anyone of you to come to me carrying over his neck a camel that will be grunting. Such a person (then) will say, 'O Muhammad! (please intercede for me).' I will say to him, 'I can't help you for I conveyed Allâh's Message to you.'" (*Sahih Al-Bukhâri, Hadith* No. 1402)

[For details about *Zakat*, please see the Book *Sahih Al-Bukhari*, the Book of *Zakât*.]

❖❖❖

Saum (Fasting)

Saum, fasting of the month of Ramadân, was enjoined during the second year of *Hijrah*.[1] The fasting in the month of Ramadân is obligatory on every sane, adult Muslim as Allâh ﷻ says:

"O you who believe! Observing *As-Saum* (the fasting) is prescribed for you as it was prescribed for those before you, that you may become *Al-Muttaqûn* (the pious). [Observing *Saum* (fasts)] for a fixed number of days, but if any of you is ill or on a journey, the same number (should be made up) from other days. And as for those who can fast with difficulty, (e.g. an old man), they have (a choice either to fast or) to feed a *Miskîn* (poor person) (for every day). But whoever does good of his own accord, it is better for him. And that you fast is better for you if only you know.[2] The month of Ramadan in

---

[1] The year, the Prophet ﷺ migrated to Al-Madinah.

[2] The provision of this Verse has been abrogated by the next Verse: 185,

which was revealed the Qur'ân, a guidance for mankind and clear proofs for the guidance and the Criterion (between right and wrong). So, whoever of you sights (the crescent on the first night of) the month (of Ramadan, i.e. is present at his home), he must observe *Saum* (fasts) that month, and whoever is ill or on a journey, the same number [of days which one did not observe *Saum* (fasts) must be made up] from other days. Allâh intends for you ease, and He does not want to make things difficult for you. (He wants that you) must complete the same number (of days), and that you must magnify Allâh [i.e. to say *Takbîr* (*Allâhu Akbar*: Allâh is the Most Great)] for having guided you so that you may be grateful to Him.[1] (V. 2:183-185)

Such fasting involves refraining from eating or drinking throughout the daily fasting hours, that is, from the crack of dawn

---

with few exceptions, i.e., very old person, or pregnancy.

[1]   (a) Narrated Talhah bin 'Ubaidullâh: A bedouin with unkempt hair came to Allâh's Messenger ﷺ and said, "O Allâh's Messenger! Inform me what Allâh has made compulsory for me as regards the *Salât* (prayers)." He replied: "You have to offer perfectly the five compulsory *Salât* (prayers) in a day and night (24 hours), unless you want to pray *Nawâfil*." The bedouin further asked, "Inform me what Allâh has made compulsory for me as regards *Saum* (fasting)." He replied, "You have to fast during the whole month of Ramadân, unless you want to fast more as *Nawâfil*." The bedouin further asked, "Tell me how much *Zakât* Allâh has enjoined on me." The narrator added: Then, Allâh's Messenger ﷺ informed him all about the laws (i.e. fundamentals) of Islâm. The bedouin then said, "By Him Who has honoured you, I will neither perform any *Nawâfil* nor will I decrease what Allâh has enjoined on me." Allâh's Messenger ﷺ said, "If he is saying the truth, he will succeed (or he will be granted Paradise)." (*Sahih Al-Bukhâri, Hadîth* No. 1891)

   (b) Narrated Abû Hurairah ؓ: Allâh's Messenger ﷺ said, "*As-Siyâm* (the fasting) is *Junnah* (protection or shield or a screen or a shelter from the Hell-fire). So, the person observing *Saum* (fasting) should avoid sexual relation with his wife and should not behave foolishly and impudently, and if somebody fights with him or abuses him, he should say to him twice, 'I am to sunset. Fasting helps develop endurance, tolerance, self-restraint and fear of Allâh . It also helps one to sympathize with less fortunate Muslims and increases the reward of charity. During the month of Ramadân, the gates of Paradise are opened, and the gates of Hell are closed. In Ramadân, there is a night that, when observed, garners a reward better than that of a thousand months of worship.

The fast begins when the new moon of the month of Ramadân is sighted and ends with the new moon of the subsequent month of Shawwâl. Its end is marked with 'Eid-ul-Fitr, literally "the Breakfast Feast." If one does not fast a day or more in Ramadân for a legitimate reason, he must make up for it after the end of Ramadân.

The following are the things that invalidate fasting:
* Willful eating, drinking or sexual intercourse during the fast.
* Menstrual or postnatal bleeding
* Induced vomiting
* Drawing blood (the donation of blood).

Eating or drinking some thing out of forgetfulness does not invalidate fasting.

---

fasting.'" The Prophet ﷺ added, "By Him in Whose Hand my soul is, the smell coming out from the mouth of a fasting person is better with Allâh تعالى than the smell of musk. (Allâh says about the fasting person), 'He has left his food, drink and desires for My sake. The Saum (fast) is for Me.* So I will reward (the fasting person) for it and the reward of good deeds is multiplied ten times.'" (Sahih Al-Bukhâri, Hadîth No. 1894)

* Although all practices of worshipping are for Allâh, here Allâh تعالى singles out Saum (fasting), because fasting cannot be practised for the sake of showing off, as nobody except Allâh can know whether one is fasting or not. Therefore, fasting is a pure performance that cannot be blemished with hypocrisy. (Fath Al-Barî, Vol. 5, Page 10)

(c) Narrated Abû Hurairah ﷺ : The Prophet ﷺ said, "Whoever does not give up lying speech false statements (i.e. telling lies) and acting on those (lies), and evil actions, then Allâh is not in need of his leaving his food and drink (i.e. Allâh will not accept his fasting*)." (Sahih Al-Bukhâri, Hadîth No. 1903)

The *Hajj* (Pilgrimage)

The *Hajj* or Pilgrimage is the fifth principle of Islam. It involves the observance and performance of certain rituals during the lunar month of Dhul-Hijjah in Makkah and certain adjacent sites. The *Hajj* is obligatory once in a lifetime for every adult, sane Muslim, who is physically and financially able to perform it. As Allâh says:

> "And perform properly (i.e. all the ceremonies according to the ways of Prophet Muhammad ﷺ), the *Hajj* and *'Umrah* (i.e. the pilgrimage to Makkah) for Allâh. But if you are prevented (from completing them), sacrifice a *Hady* (animal, i.e. a sheep, a cow, or a camel) such as you can afford, and do not shave your heads until the *Hady* reaches the place of

sacrifice. And whosoever of you is ill or has an ailment in his scalp (necessitating shaving), he must pay a *Fidyah* (ransom) of either observing *Saum* (fasts) (three days) or giving *Sadaqah* (charity – feeding six poor persons) or offering sacrifice (one sheep). Then if you are in safety and whosoever performs the '*Umrah* in the months of *Hajj*, before (performing) the *Hajj*, (i.e. *Hajj-at-Tamattu*' and *Al-Qirân*), he must slaughter a *Hady* such as he can afford, but if he cannot afford it, he should observe Saum (fasts) three days during the *Hajj* and seven days after his return (to his home), making ten days in all. This is for him whose family is not present at *Al-Masjid Al-Harâm* (i.e. non-resident of Makkah). And fear Allâh much and know that Allâh is Severe in punishment." (V. 2:196)[1]

Narrated Abu Hurairah ﷺ that Allâh's Messenger ﷺ said: "Whoever performs *Hajj* to this House (Ka'bah) and does not approach his wife for sexual relations nor commits sins (while performing *Hajj*), he will come out as sinless as a newly born child (just delivered by his mother)." (*Sahih Al-Bukhari, Hadith* No. 1819)

Islam demolishes all the previous evil deeds and so do migration (for Allâh's sake) and *Hajj* (pilgrimage to Makkah). [*Al-Lu'lu' Wal-Marjân*, Vol. 1, Ch.52]

---

[1]   Islâm demolishes all the previous evil deeds and so do migration (for Allâh's sake) and *Hajj* (pilgrimage to Makkah). [*Al-Lu'lu' wal-Marjân*, Vol. 1, Ch.52]. The obligation of performing '*Umrah* and its superiority. Ibn 'Umar عنهما رضى الله said, "*Hajj* and '*Umrah* are obligatory for everybody." And Ibn 'Abbâs عنهما رضى الله said, "*Umrah* is mentioned in conjunction with *Hajj* in the Book of Allâh : 'And perform properly *Hajj* and '*Umrah* for Allâh.'" (V. 2:196)

Narrated Abu Hurairah ﷺ: Allâh's Messenger ﷺ said, "(The performance of) '*Umrah* is an expiation for the sins committed (between it and the previous one). And the reward of *Hajj Mabrûr* (the one accepted by Allâh) is nothing except Paradise." (*Sahih Al-Bukhâri, Hadîth* No.1773)

The obligation of performing 'Umrah and its superiority

Ibn 'Umar رضى الله عنهما said, "Hajj and 'Umrah are obligatory for everybody." And Ibn 'Abbâs رضى الله عنهما said, "Umrah is mentioned in conjunction with Hajj in the Book of Allâh ﷺ:

'And perform properly Hajj and 'Umrah for Allâh ﷺ.'" (V. 2: 196)

Narrated Abu Hurairah ﷺ that Allâh's Messenger ﷺ said:

"(The performance of) 'Umrah is an expiation for the sins committed (between it and the previous one). And the reward of Hajj Mabrûr (the one accepted by Allâh) is nothing except Paradise." (Sahih Al-Bukhâri, Hadîth No. 1773)

Like any other act of worship, the performance of the Hajj must be preceded with the intention to do it, by saying Labbaik [for pilgrimage (Hajj or Umrah) arriving there for the Miqat (place prescribed by the Prophet ﷺ for each country) while coming to Makkah]. It also requires the wearing of a garment of consecration, Ihrâm.[1] In fact, the donning of such clothing is a concrete form of expressing the intention for the Hajj or an 'Umrah,[2] the Lesser Pilgrimage. Once a person enters the state of consecration and puts on the garment, which consists of a large

---

[1] Ihrâm, or consecration, is entering upon a state intending for the performance of the Hajj or an 'Umrah (the Lesser Pilgrimage). For a man, this involves wrapping one piece of unsewn cloth round the body from above the navel to below the knees. Another piece is wrapped over his upper body except for the head. It is unlawful for him to put on sewn garments, socks or shoes. Only slippers or the like are permitted as footwear. Also prohibited are all sexual activities with one's wife, hunting and the like. Under normal circumstances, once a Muslim enters the state of consecration, he may not break it till he has completed all the Hajj and 'Umrah rituals. But if one is held back from completing the Hajj or an 'Umrah for health reasons, fear of an enemy or great danger, he may quit his state of consecration and sacrifice a sheep, a goat, cow or camel in expiation.

[2] 'Umrah, often called the Lesser Pilgrimage in English, is a visit to Makkah at any time of year. Its rituals take place entirely within the precincts of the Sacred Mosque of Makkah. 'Umrah is also usually a part

cloth to cover the upper part of the body and another to cover the body from the navel down. The following things become prohibited until the state of consecration is terminated by the end of *Hajj* or *'Umrah*:

1. Trimming or plucking hair from any part of the body,
2. Clipping fingernails or toenails,
3. Wearing a hat or other head covering,
4. Wearing perfume,
5. Consummating a marriage, and
6. Sexual intercourse.

The pilgrimage begins with seven circuits of the Ka'bah and continues with crossing the distance between the two hills of Safa and Marwah. On the 8th of the month of Dhul-Hijjah, the pilgrims move on to Mina, then to Arafât, then Muzdalifah, then back to Mina to perform certain rituals and end the procedure with the sacrifice of an animal, either a sheep, a goat, a cow or a camel. [For details about the *Hajj*, please see the Book *Sahih Al-Bukhari* (in the Book of *Hajj*).]

---

of the *Hajj*. It includes seven circuits of the *Ka'bah*, followed by two units or *Rak'ât* of prayer, the drinking of water of the well of *Zamzam* and finally, the crossing of the distance between the hills of Safa and Marwah seven times, and cutting of some of one's hair.

The Articles of Faith

There are six articles of Faith:

1. Belief in Allâh ﷻ,
2. Belief in His Angels,
3. Belief in His Books,
4. Belief in His Messengers,
5. Belief in the Last Day (the Day of Resurrection and Hereafter) and
6. Belief in the Divine Preordainment and Divine Decrees (*Qadâ'* and *Qadar*).

Belief in Allâh ﷻ

To believe in Allâh ﷻ means declaring Allâh to be the only God, in heavens and earth and all that exists, to whom worship is due, that He is the Creator of everything and the Sustainer of everything, that it is He Who gives life and causes death, and that He is Unique in His Names and Attributes.

Belief in His Angels

Allâh ﷻ has created the angels from light. They are honorable slaves of Allâh , who obey Him and execute His Commands. Allâh ﷻ describes them:

"Who disobey not, (from executing) the Commands they receive from Allâh, but do that which they are commanded." (V. 66:6)

Allâh ﷻ created them to worship Him, and only Allâh knows how many they are. Among them are:

* Gabriel who is charged with delivering Divine revelations to the Prophets and Messengers of Allâh ﷻ,
* Michael who is charged with the rain,
* The angel of death who is charged with collecting human souls,
* The bearers of the Throne of Allâh ﷻ, and
* The guards of Paradise and Hell.

Beside these, there are angels who guard humans, others who record people's deeds and utterances and still others who are charged with various other duties and tasks.

Belief in His Books

Belief in His Books is believing that Allâh the Exalted did reveal Books to His Messengers to convey them to their people. Those Books comprise the Speech of Allâh ﷻ. These were doubtlessly chaste at the point of revelation, and whenever a Book or Scripture was revealed, it abrogated the preceding one. The known Divine Scriptures are:

The Torah, the Book Allâh ﷻ, revealed to Moses عليه السلام; the Psalms, the Book revealed to David عليه السلام; the Gospel, revealed to Jesus عليه السلام. The Books in the hands of the Christians and Jews today, that is, the Torah and the Bible with the Old Testament and the New Testament are not authentic because they have been distorted, altered and tampered with. Moreover, they were abrogated by the last of Allâh's Books, the Qur'ân.

The Qur'ân, it is the Word of Allâh ﷻ, His final Book for mankind, which Allâh ﷻ revealed to Muhammad ﷺ the last of His Prophets and Messengers to be sent to mankind. Allâh ﷻ sent it down to make everything clear and as a means of guidance and mercy. Allâh ﷻ has promised to preserve and guard it against distortion, adulteration, addition or harm. He says:

"Verily, We, it is We Who have sent down the *Dhikr* (i.e. the Qur'ân), and surely We will guard it (from corruption)." (V. 15:9)

This Verse is a challenge to mankind and everyone is obliged to believe in the miracles of this Qur'ân. It is a clear fact that more than 1400 years have elapsed and not a single word of this Qur'ân has been changed, although the disbelievers tried their utmost to change it in every way, but they failed miserably in their efforts. As it is mentioned in this holy Verse: "We will guard it." By Allâh! He has guarded it. On the contrary, all the other holy Books [the Taurât (Torah), the Injîl (Gospel)] have been corrupted in the form of additions or subtractions or alterations in the original text.

The Qur'ân was revealed to the Prophet Muhammad ﷺ in portions as circumstances warranted, over a period of twenty-three years, thirteen of which were in Makkah and ten in Al-Madinah. It is divided into 114 *Sûrahs* (chapters) of varying length.

Belief in His Messengers

Muslims attest that Allâh ﷻ did send Messengers to every nation inviting them to worship Him Alone. This belief also entails the denouncement of all gods that are worshiped besides Allâh ﷻ or instead of Him, and the assertion that all Messengers were truthful and discharged their duty in the best manner. Allâh ﷻ sent many Messengers, and only Allâh ﷻ knows how many. It is incumbent upon all Muslims to believe in all the Prophets and Messengers. He who denies one of them denies all. The first Messenger Allâh ﷻ sent to mankind was Noah عليه السلام, and the last was Muhammad ﷺ. Allâh ﷻ says:

> "And verily, We have sent among every *Ummah* (community, nation) a Messenger (proclaiming): 'Worship Allâh (Alone), and avoid (or keep away from) *Tâghût*.'"[1] (V. 16:36)

---

[1]   The word *Tâghût* covers a wide range of meanings: It means anything worshiped other than the Real God (Allâh), but the one who does not accept to be worshiped, will not be considered as a *Tâghût*, i.e., all the false deities. It may be satan, devils, idols, stones, sun, stars, angels, human beings, who were falsely worshiped and taken as *Tâghût*. Likewise saints, graves, rulers and leaders are falsely worshiped and wrongly followed. Sometimes *Tâghût* means a false judge who gives a false judgement.

All Prophets and Messengers were human beings. Allâh ﷻ distinguished them by commissioning them as Prophets and Messengers and supported them with miracles. They had no Divine qualities, and had no access to the Unseen world. But Allâh ﷻ sent Muhammad ﷺ to all mankind saying:

"Say (O Muhammad ﷺ): 'O mankind! Verily, I am sent to you all as the Messenger of Allâh.'" (V. 7:158)

Of all the Messengers, there are five who were the most persevering and determined to do what Allâh ﷻ had enjoined them. They were Noah, Abraham, Moses, Jesus and Muhammad ﷺ, who was the last and the best of them all and remains the best of all human beings.

Allâh ﷻ said:

"And Messengers We have mentioned to you before, and Messengers We have not mentioned to you, – and to Mûsâ (Moses) Allâh spoke directly. Messengers as bearers of good news as well as of warning in order that mankind should have no plea against Allâh after the (coming of) Messengers. And Allâh is Ever All-Powerful, All-Wise." (V. 4: 164, 165)

Allâh ﷻ said:

"It is those who believe (in the Oneness of Allâh and worship none but Him Alone) and confuse not their Belief with *Zulm*[1] (wrong, i.e. by worshipping others besides Allâh), for them (only) there is security and they are the

---

[1] Narrated 'Abdullâh ﷺ: When the following Verse was revealed: "It is those who believe (in the Oneness of Allâh and worship none but Him Alone) and confuse not their belief with *Zulm* (wrong, i.e., by worshiping others besides Allâh.)..." (V.6:82), the Companions of Allâh's Messenger said, "Who is amongst us who had not done *Zulm* (wrong)?" Then Allâh revealed: "Verily, joining others in worship with Allâh is a great *Zulm* (wrong) indeed." (V.31:13) (*Sahih Al-Bukhari, Hadith* No. 32)

guided. And that was Our Proof which We gave Ibrâhîm (Abraham) against his people. We raise whom We will in degrees. Certainly your Lord is All-Wise, All-Knowing. And We bestowed upon him Ishâq (Isaac) and Ya'qûb (Jacob), each of them We guided, and before him, We guided Nûh (Noah), and among his progeny Dâwûd (David), Sulaimân (Solomon), Ayyub (Job), Yûsuf (Joseph), Mûsâ (Moses), and Hârûn (Aaron). Thus do We reward Al-Muhsinûn."[1] And Zakariyyâ (Zechariah), and Yahyâ (John) and 'Îsâ (Jesus) and Ilyâs (Elias), each one of them was of the righteous. And Ismâ'îl (Ishmael) and Al-Yasa'a (Elisha), and Yûnus (Jonah) and Lût (Lot), and each one of them We preferred above the 'Âlamîn [mankind and jinn (of their times)]. And also some of their fathers and their progeny and their brethren, We chose them, and We guided them to the Straight Path. This is the Guidance of Allâh with which He guides whomsoever He wills of His slaves. But if they had joined in worship others with Allâh, all that they used to do would have been of no benefit to them. They are those whom We gave the Book, Al-Hukm (understanding of the religious laws), and Prophethood. But if these disbelieve therein (the Book, Al-Hukm and Prophethood), then indeed We have entrusted it to a people (such as the Companions of Prophet Muhammad ﷺ) who are not disbelievers therein. They are those whom Allâh had guided. So follow their guidance. Say: 'No reward I ask of you for this (the Qur'ân). It is only a reminder for the 'Âlamîn (mankind and jinn).' They (the Jews, Quraish pagans, idolaters) did not estimate Allâh with an estimation due to Him when they said: 'Nothing did Allâh send down to any human being (by Revelation).' Say

---

[1] *Muhsinûn*: Doers of good, i.e., those who perform good deeds totally for Allâh's sake only without any show-off or to gain praise or fame and they do them in accordance with the *Sunnah* (legal ways) of Allâh's Messenger, Muhammad ﷺ.

(O Muhammad ﷺ): 'Who then sent down the Book which Mûsâ (Moses) brought, a light and a guidance to mankind which you (the Jews) have made into (separate) paper sheets, disclosing (some of it) and concealing (much). And you (believers in Allâh and His Messenger Muhammad ﷺ) were taught (through the Qur'ân) that which neither you nor your fathers knew.' Say: 'Allâh (sent it down).' Then leave them to play in their vain discussions. And this (the Qur'ân) is a blessed Book which We have sent down, confirming (the Revelations) which came before it, so that you may warn the Mother of Towns (i.e. Makkah) and all those around it. Those who believe in the Hereafter believe in it (the Qur'ân), and they are constant in guarding their *Salât* (prayers)." (V. 6: 82-92)

Belief in the Last Day (the Day of Resurrection and Hereafter)

The one whose bad deeds outweigh his good ones, will be condemned to Hell-fire. Islam is a precondition for the acceptance of any good deed.

There are minor and major signs of the Final Hour. Nearly all of the minor signs have appeared. They include the mission of the Prophet Muhammad ﷺ, swift passing of time and the competition of the shepherds in the erection of tall buildings, as well as the prevalence of liquor consumption, fornication and many other vices.

The major signs will include the advent of the Antichrist, an impostor who will claim to be god. He will traverse throughout the earth but will not be able to enter Makkah nor Al-Madinah. The descent of Jesus عليه السلام from heaven is a second major sign. He will kill the Antichrist (*Masih Ad-Dajjal*), kill the swine and do other deeds. A third is the emergence of Gog and Magog people, two large human nations who will devastate the earth, whom Allâh will finally cause to die.

The last major sign signaling the end of all creatures and creations will be the rising of the sun from the west. The first blow of a horn will mark the end. All creatures will be raised to assemble for the Day of Reckoning beginning with the second blow. That Day will last for 50,000 years during which humans will remain standing, naked and uncircumcised, the way they were born. As a result, they will suffer greatly and will sink in their own perspiration each according to his evil deeds. Some will be sinking up to their ankles, some to their knees, some to their waists, some to their breasts, and yet some up to their mouths. None of the Messengers will be able to help his own people. But mankind will ask Muhammad ﷺ to intercede on their behalf after being turned down by the other gracious Messengers. He will intercede with Allâh ﷻ on their behalf so that the reckoning may begin. Allâh ﷻ will approve his intercession.

After the accounting, everyone will receive his record. Those who receive theirs with their right hands will prosper and be admitted to Paradise, while those who receive their record with their left hands, or from behind their backs, will be doomed to misery. A bridge, thinner than a whisker and sharper than a razor, will be set over Hell. Every one must cross the bridge, some will be able to make it safely, while the rest will fall into Hell.

The Description of Paradise

Paradise, *Jannah* in Arabic, is the abode that Allâh ﷻ has prepared for believers. It holds means of everlasting bliss no eye has seen, no ear heard or human imagined. In it are pure female mates, rivers of milk, rivers of wine, rivers of pure honey and every kind of delicious fruit and meat. Its residents will not experience exhaustion, boredom or death.

The Description of Hell

Hell-fire is the abode Allâh ﷻ has prepared for the disbelievers in the Oneness of Allâh who deny Him and His Messengers. Its food is intolerantly bitter, and its drink is the pus exuding from the skins of its inmates. Its depth is unfathomable. The disbelievers in the Oneness of Allâh and the hypocrites will live in it forever.

> **Belief in *Qadâ'* and *Qadar* (the Divine Preordainment and Divine Decrees) i.e. whatever Allâh has ordained must come to pass**

Doom (*Qadâ'*) is the general Decree of Allâh ﷻ that every human shall die, whereas a Divine Decree (*Qadar*) is a particular Decree of Allâh ﷻ, or the execution of *Qadâ'*, that certain person is to die at a particular time and place. Hence believing in this article entails believing that Allâh ﷻ has created everything and has foreordained its proper measure.

The Facets of *Qadar*

1. Allâh ﷻ is well acquainted with everything taking place, and His Knowledge encompasses everything.

2. Allâh ﷻ has preassigned portions of everything in the Preserved Tablet(اللوح المحفوظ) .

3. Nothing takes place in the heavens or on the earth without the Will of Allâh ﷻ and His Wish. Whatever Allâh ﷻ wills, takes place and whatever He does not will, does not take place.

4. Allâh ﷻ is the Creator of all things. There is no other creator beside Him.

﴿ءَامَنَ ٱلرَّسُولُ بِمَآ أُنزِلَ إِلَيْهِ مِن رَّبِّهِ وَٱلْمُؤْمِنُونَ كُلٌّ ءَامَنَ بِٱللَّهِ وَمَلَٰٓئِكَتِهِ وَكُتُبِهِ وَرُسُلِهِ لَا نُفَرِّقُ بَيْنَ أَحَدٍ مِّن رُّسُلِهِ وَقَالُوا سَمِعْنَا وَأَطَعْنَا غُفْرَانَكَ رَبَّنَا وَإِلَيْكَ ٱلْمَصِيرُ﴾

"The Messenger (Muhammad ﷺ) believes in what has been sent down to him from his Lord, and (so do) the believers. Each one believes in Allâh, His Angels, His Books, and His Messengers. (They say,) 'We make no distinction between one another of His Messengers' and they say, 'We hear, and we obey. (We seek) your Forgiveness, our Lord, and to You is the return (of all).'"
(V. 2:285)

The Rules and Regulations of Hygiene in Islam

Islamic legal orders deal with the personal as well as social life of a man to ensure his purity and cleanliness in his body, clothing, food, environment, behavior, manners, thoughts and intentions.

The rules and regulations of hygiene in Islam appears unique when it is compared with those of other religions. In Islam, hygiene is not considered a matter of personal discretion. Rather, the ablution (*Wudû'*) is obligatory, a pre-condition for a ritual prayer. A Muslim has to offer at least five obligatory prayers every day with purity in his heart and mind and cleanliness in his body and clothes. The prayer is also to be offered with a pure intention, on a pure spot. One can easily understand the beneficial effects and results a Muslim can gain by the repetition of the act. It is also obligatory to have a bath, subsequent to sexual intercourse, after a menstrual period and on some other occasions.

Required in addition to these acts of hygiene, are cleaning the teeth to prevent tooth decay, gum disease and halitosis; clipping fingernails and toenails; trimming the mustache, as well as shaving the hair of the pubes and the armpits. All of these requirements prove that Islam not only deals with man's spiritual needs, but also with his physical health.

Islam has honored women by charging them with the raising of future generations. Before Islam, a woman was treated as a household object, deprived of her rights to the point that the eldest son would even inherit his father's wives. Female infants used to be buried alive during the pre-Islamic era. Other cultures also used to consider women as less than human.

Not only does Islam honor women, but it also deems her equal to man in terms of accomplishments and requital. Allâh ﷻ has set piety, not sex, as a criterion of superiority. He says:

"O mankind! We have created you from a male and a female, and made you into nations and tribes that you may know one another. Verily, the most honorable of you with Allâh is that (believer) who has *At-Taqwâ* [he is one of the *Muttaqûn* [the pious believers of Islamic Monotheism who fear Allâh much (abstain from all kinds of sins and evil deeds which He has forbidden) and love Allâh much (perform all kinds of good deeds which He has ordained)]." (V. 49:13)

Allâh ﷻ entitled her to own property and the right to dispose of it at her own discretion, as she knows she is responsible before Allâh ﷻ. A husband has no right to claim any of the property of his wife unless she gives whatever she wants to him, willingly. Moreover, Allâh ﷻ grants parents in general a grand status by commanding children to be kind to them saying:

"And your Lord has decreed that you worship none but Him. And that you be dutiful to your parents. If one of them or both of them attain old age in your life, say not to them a word of disrespect, nor shout at them but address them in terms of honour." (V. 17:23)

Allâh ﷻ has commanded that He Alone should be worshiped and with this command, commanded children to treat parents kindly. The Verse shows the honorable status of parents in Islam. The mother, however, deserves greater respect and kindness as shown by the following tradition:

A man asked Allâh's Messenger ﷺ, "Who deserves my kind company most?" He said, "Your mother." He further asked, "Then who?" He said, "Your mother," and he repeated the same question two more times, and the Prophet ﷺ gave the same answer. The fourth time he said, "Your father."

The Dress Code for Women

Among non-Muslims, the issue of a woman's clothing is controversial. The controversy arises from their ignorance of Islam and its principles. They assume that the Muslim woman is trapped in her home, deprived of her rights. They view the Muslim woman from the historical perspective of their own culture, in which woman has rebelled against its oppression and liberated herself from the shackles of the past. This is rather the ethnocentric thinking of non-Muslim women. This is due to the fact that Western women have neither in the past nor at present experienced the true sense of liberation.

From ancient times through the Middle Ages, the Renaissance and the Industrial Revolution to the present age of technology, they have moved from one form of slavery into another, of their own free will, thinking the latest stage is the ultimate liberation, when it is only slavery in a new disguise. They have come out of their homes to elbow their way into the male crowd demanding equality, ignoring the fact that their physiques have certain limits and that they are endowed with certain functions for certain objectives. The results can be seen clearly in the devastation of the Western family.

The woman's wearing of a veil in Islam is not a cultural custom, inherited from a more ancient culture or civilization. Rather, it is an institution commanded by Allâh the One Who created mankind. Due to His infinite wisdom, He enjoined it on women.

As Allâh's Statement:

"O Prophet! Tell your wives and your daughters and the women of the believers to draw their cloaks (veils) all over their bodies (i.e. Screen themselves completely except the eyes or one eye to see the way). That will be better that they should be known (as free respectable women) so as not to be annoyed. And Allâh is Ever Oft-Forgiving, Most Merciful." (V. 33:59)

Narrated 'Âishah رضي الله عنها "May Allâh bestow His Mercy on the early emigrant women. When Allâh revealed: 'And to draw their veils all over *Juyûbihinna* (i.e. their bodies, faces, necks, and bosoms)' – they tore their *Murûts* (a woollen dress, or a waist-binding cloth or an apron) and covered their heads and faces with those torn *Murûts*." (*Sahih Al-Bukhari, Hadith* No. 4758)

Narrated Safiyyah bint Shaibah that 'Âishah رضي الله عنها used to say:

"When the Verse: 'And to draw their veils all over *Juyûbihinna* (i.e. their bodies, faces, necks, and bosoms)' (V.24: 31) was revealed, (the ladies) cut their waist sheets at the edges and covered their heads and faces with those cut pieces of cloth.'" (*Sahih Al-Bukhari, Hadith* No. 4759)

Both man and woman are created with sexual desires. Allâh has laid down certain regulations and precautionary measures to curtail these desires and to guard each sex against all forms of illicit relations for the preservation of posterity and for the maintenance of a proper relationship between a man and a woman. The observance of those regulations and precautions will lead to the establishment of a healthy family and a healthy community.

"This is the Book (the Qur'ân), whereof there is no doubt, a guidance to those who are *Al-Muttaqûn* [the pious believers of Islamic Monotheism who fear Allâh much (abstain from all kinds of sins and evil deeds which He has forbidden) and love Allâh much (perform all kinds of good deeds which He has ordained)]." (V. 2:2)

"And this (submission to Allâh, Islam) was enjoined by Ibrâhîm (Abraham) upon his sons and by Ya'qûb (Jacob) (saying), "O my sons! Allâh has chosen for you the (true) religion, then die not except in the Faith of Islam (as Muslims – Islamic Monotheism)." (V. 2:132)

"And whoever seeks a religion other than Islam, it will never be accepted of him, and in the Hereafter he will be one of the losers." (V. 3:85)

"This day, I have perfected your religion for you, completed My Favor upon you, and have chosen for you Islam as your religion." (V. 5:3)

"Verily, those who disbelieve in Allâh and His Messengers and wish to make distinction between Allâh and His Messengers (by believing in Allâh and disbelieving in His Messengers) saying, 'We believe in some but reject others,' and wish to adopt a way in between. They are in truth disbelievers. And We have prepared for the disbelievers a humiliating torment." (V. 4:150,151)

"It is He Who has sent His Messenger (Muhammad ﷺ) with guidance and the religion of truth (Islam), to make it superior over all religions even though the *Mushrikûn* (polytheists, pagans, idolaters, disbelievers in the Oneness of Allâh) hate (it)." (V. 9:33)

"Is he whose breast Allâh has opened to Islam, so that he is in light from his Lord (as he who is a non-Muslim)? So, woe to those whose hearts are hardened against remembrance of Allâh! They are in plain error!" (V. 39:22)

"He it is Who has sent His Messenger (Muhammad ﷺ) with guidance and the religion of truth (Islam), that He may make it (Islam) superior to all religions. And All-Sufficient is Allâh as a Witness." (V. 48:28)

"O mankind! Worship your Lord (Allâh), Who created you and those who were before you so that you may become *Al-Muttaqûn* [the pious believers of Islamic Monotheism who fear Allâh much (abstain from all kinds of sins and evil deeds which He has forbidden) and love Allâh much (perform all kinds of good deeds which He has ordained)]." (V. 2:21)

"Who has made the earth a resting place for you, and the sky as a canopy, and sent down water (rain) from the sky and brought forth therewith fruits as a provision for you. Then do not set up rivals to Allâh (in worship) while you know (that He Alone has the right to be worshipped)." (V. 2:22)[1]

---

[1] Narrated 'Abdullâh ﷺ: I asked the Prophet ﷺ, "What is the greatest sin in consideration with Allâh?" He said, "That you set up a rival unto Allâh though He Alone created you." I said, "That is indeed a great sin." Then I asked, "What is next?" He said, "To kill your son lest he should share your food with you." I asked, "What is next?" He said, "To commit illegal sexual intercourse with the wife of your neighbour." (*Sahih Al-Bukhâri, Hadîth* No. 4477)

Narrated 'Abdullâh bin 'Amr ﷺ: A man asked the Prophet ﷺ, "What qualities of Islam are good." The Prophet ﷺ replied, "To feed (others) and to greet those whom you know and those whom you do not know." (*Sahih Al-Bukhâri, Hadith* No. 12)

Narrated Abu Sa'îd Al-Khudrî ﷺ: Allâh's Messenger ﷺ said, "If a person embraces Islam sincerely, then Allâh shall forgive all his past sins, and after that starts the settlement of accounts, the reward of his good deeds will be ten times to seven hundred times for each good deed and an evil deed will be recorded as it is, unless Allâh forgives it." (*Sahih Al-Bukhâri, Hadith* No. 41)

Narrated Abu Hurairah ﷺ: Allâh's Messenger ﷺ said, "Every child is born on *Fitrah* [true faith of Islamic Monotheism (i.e. to worship none but Allâh Alone)] but his parents convert him to Judaism, Christianity or Magianism, as an animal gives birth to a perfect baby animal. Do you find it mutilated?" Then Abu Hurairah ﷺ recited the holy Verses: "Allâh's *Fitrah* with which He has created mankind. No change let there be in *Khalqillah* (i.e., the religion of Allâh – Islamic Monotheism): that is the Straight Religion (Islam) (V. 30:30)." (*Sahih Al-Bukhâri, Hadith* No. 1359)

Narrated Abu Hurairah ﷺ: Allâh's Messenger ﷺ said, "All my followers will enter Paradise except those who refuse." They (the people) asked, "O Allâh's Messenger! Who will refuse?" He said, "Whoever obeys me will enter Paradise, and whoever disobeys me is the one who refuses (to enter it)." (*Sahih Al-Bukhâri, Hadith* No. 7280)

The Statement of the Prophet ﷺ: "Religion is *An-Nasîhah* (to be sincere and true) to: (1) Allâh ﷺ [i.e. obeying Him, by following

His religion of Islamic Monotheism, attributing to Him what He deserves and doing *Jihâd* for His sake and to believe in Him, to fear Him much (abstain from all kinds of sins and evil deeds which He has forbidden) and love Him much (perform all kinds of good deeds which He has ordained)]; (2) to Allâh's Messenger [i.e. to respect him greatly and to believe that he (ﷺ) is Allâh's Messenger, and to fight on his behalf both in his lifetime and after his death and to follow his *Sunnah* – (legal ways etc.)]; (3) to the Muslim rulers (i.e. to help them in their job of leading Muslims to the right path and alarm them if they are heedless); and (4) to all the Muslims (in common) [i.e. to order them for *Al-Ma'rûf* (i.e. Islamic Monotheism, and all that Islam orders one to do), and to forbid them from *Al-Munkar* (i.e. disbelief, polytheism of all kinds, and all that Islam has forbidden), and to be merciful and kind to them].

Narrated Jarîr bin Abdullâh ؓ: I gave the *Bai'ah* (pledge) to Allâh's Messenger ﷺ for the following:

1. *Iqâmat-as-Salât* (to perform prayers).

2. To pay the *Zakât*.

3. And to be sincere and true to every Muslim [i.e. to order them for *Al-Ma'rûf* (i.e. Islamic Monotheism, and all that Islam orders one to do), and to forbid them from *Al-Munkar* (i.e. disbelief, polytheism of all kinds, and all that Islam has forbidden), and to help them, and to be merciful and kind to them]. (*Sahih Al-Bukhâri, Hadith* No. 57 and its chapter No. 42)

Biblical Prophecy on the Advent of Muhammad ﷺ

John 14: 15-16 –

"If you love me, keep my commandments. And I will pray the Father and He shall give you another Comforter that he may abide with you forever."

John 15:26-27 –

"But when the Comforter is come, whom I will send unto you from the Father, even the Spirit of Truth, which proceedeth from the Father, he shall testify of me: And ye also shall bear witness, because ye have been with me from the beginning."

John 16:5-8 –

"But now I go my way to Him that sent me and none of you asked me, 'Whither goest thou? But because I have said these things unto you, sorrow hath filled your heart. Nevertheless I tell you the truth; for if I go not away, the Comforter will not come unto you; but if I depart, I will send him unto you. And when he is come, he will reprove the world of sin, and approve righteousness and judgment."

John 16:12-14 –

"I have yet many things to say unto you, but you cannot bear them now. How be it when he, the Spirit of Truth, is come, he will guide you into all truth: for he shall not speak of himself; but whatsoever he shall hear, that shall he speak; and he will shew you things to come. He shall glorify me: for he shall receive of mine, and he shall shew it unto you."

John 16:16 –

"A little while and ye shall not see me: and again a little while, ye shall see me, because I go to the Father."

[Muslim theologians have stated that the person who is described by Jesus to come after him in the above verses does not comply with any other person but Muhammad ﷺ, the Messenger of Allâh. This 'person' whom Jesus prophesied will come after him, is called in the Bible 'Parqaleeta.' This word was deleted by later interpreters and translators and changed at times to 'Spirit of Truth', and at other times, to 'Comforter' and sometimes to 'Holy Spirit'. The original word is Greek and its meaning is 'one whom people praise exceedingly.' The sense of the word is applicable to the word 'Muhammad' (in Arabic).]

﴿وَإِذْ قَالَ عِيسَى ٱبْنُ مَرْيَمَ يَٰبَنِىٓ إِسْرَٰٓءِيلَ إِنِّى رَسُولُ ٱللَّهِ إِلَيْكُم مُّصَدِّقًا لِّمَا بَيْنَ يَدَىَّ مِنَ ٱلتَّوْرَىٰةِ وَمُبَشِّرًا بِرَسُولٍ يَأْتِى مِنۢ بَعْدِى ٱسْمُهُۥٓ أَحْمَدُ﴾

"And (remember) When 'Îsâ (Jesus), son of Maryam (Mary), said: 'O Children of Israel! I am the Messenger of Allâh to you, confirming the Taurât [(Torah) which came] before me, and giving glad tidings of a Messenger to come after me, whose name shall be Ahmad.'" (V. 61:6)

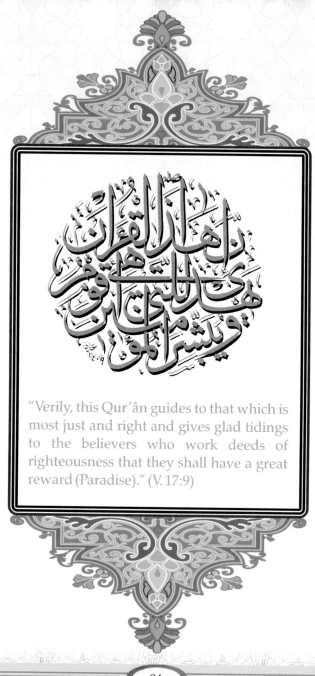

"Verily, this Qur'ân guides to that which is most just and right and gives glad tidings to the believers who work deeds of righteousness that they shall have a great reward (Paradise)." (V. 17:9)

Allâh's Statements

Who created the Universe

"Blessed is He (Allâh) Who has placed in the heaven big stars, and has placed therein a great lamp (sun), and a moon giving light. And He (Allâh) it is Who has put the night and the day in succession, for such who desires to remember or desires to show his gratitude." (V. 25: 61,62)

Who are the Best People

"And the (faithful) slaves of the Most Gracious (Allâh) are those who walk on the earth in humility and sedateness, and when the foolish address them (with bad words) they reply back with mild words of gentleness. And those who spend the night in worship of their Lord, prostrate and standing.[1] And those who say: 'Our Lord! Avert from us the torment of Hell. Verily, its torment is ever an inseparable, permanent punishment.' Evil indeed it (Hell) is as an abode and as a place to rest in. And those who, when they spend, are neither extravagant nor niggardly, but hold a medium (way) between those (extremes)." (V. 25: 63-67)

"And those who invoke not any other *ilâh* (god) along with Allâh, nor kill such person as Allâh has forbidden, except for just cause, nor commit illegal sexual intercourse – and whoever does this, shall receive the punishment.[2] The torment will be doubled

---

[1] Ibn 'Abbâs رضى الله عنهما said: "Whosoever prayed two *Rak'at* (units of prayer) or more after the *'Isha* (night) prayer, will be considered like those mentioned in this Verse." And Al-Kalabi said: "Whosoever prayed two *Rak'at* after the *Maghrib* (evening) prayer, and four *Rak'at* after the *'Ishâ* (night) prayer will be considered like those mentioned in this Verse." (*Tafsîr Al-Qurtubî*)

[2] a) Narrated 'Abdullâh ﷺ: I asked the Prophet ﷺ, "What is the greatest sin in consideration with Allâh?" He said, "That you set up a rival unto Allâh though

to him on the Day of Resurrection, and he will abide therein in disgrace; Except those who repent and believe (in Islamic Monotheism), and do righteous deeds; for those, Allâh will change their sins into good deeds, and Allâh is Ever-Forgiving, Most Merciful.[1] And whosoever repents and does righteous good deeds; then verily, he repents towards Allâh with true repentance." (V. 25:68-71)

"And those who do not bear witness to falsehood, and if they pass by some evil play or evil talk, they pass by it with dignity. And those who, when they are reminded of the *Ayât* (proofs, evidences, verses, lessons, signs, revelations, etc.) of their Lord, fall not deaf and blind thereat. And those who say: 'Our Lord! Bestow on us from our wives and our offspring the comfort of our eyes, and make us leaders of the *Muttaqûn* (the pious).' Those will be rewarded with the highest place (in Paradise) because of their patience. Therein

---

He Alone created you." I said, "That is indeed a great sin." Then I asked, "What is next?" He said, "To kill your son lest he should share your food with you." I asked, "What is next?" He said, "To commit illegal sexual intercourse with the wife of your neighbour." (*Sahîh Al-Bukhâri, Hadîth* No. 4477)

b) Narrated Anas ﷺ: The Prophet ﷺ was asked about the great sins. He said, "They are:

a) To join others in worship with Allâh.

b) To be undutiful to one's parents.

c) To kill a person (which Allâh has forbidden to be killed, i.e., to commit the crime of murdering).

d) And to give a false witness." (*Sahîh Al-Bukhâri, Hadîth* No. 2653)

[1] Islam demolishes all the previous evil deeds and so do migration (for Allâh's sake) and *Hajj* (pilgrimage to Makkah). (*Al-Lu'lu' wal-Marjân*, Vol. 1, Chapter 52)

Narrated Ibn 'Abbâs رضى الله عنهما: Some pagans who committed murders in great number and committed illegal sexual intercourse excessively, came to Muhammad ﷺ and said: "O Muhammad! Whatever you say, and invite people to, is good, but we wish if you could inform us whether we can make an expiation for our (past evil) deeds." So the Divine Verses came: "Those who invoke not any other *ilâh* (god) along with Allâh, nor kill such person as Allâh has forbidden except for just cause, nor commit illegal sexual intercourse." (V.25:68) "... Except those who repent..."

they shall be met with greetings and the word of peace and respect. Abiding therein – excellent it is as an abode, and as a place to rest in. Say (O Muhammad ﷺ to the disbelievers): 'My Lord pays attention to you only because of your invocation to Him. But now you have indeed denied (Him). So the torment will be yours for ever (inseparable, permanent punishment).'" (V. 25: 72-77)

About those who turn away from the Messengers

"And (remember) when Mûsâ (Moses) said to his people: 'O my people! Why do you annoy me while you know certainly that I am the Messenger of Allâh to you?' So, when they turned away (from the path of Allâh), Allâh turned their hearts away (from the Right Path). And Allâh guides not the people who are Fâsiqûn (rebellious, disobedient to Allâh). And (remember) when 'Isâ (Jesus), son of Maryam (Mary), said: 'O Children of Israel! I am the Messenger of Allâh to you, confirming the Taurât [(Torah) which came] before me, and giving glad tidings of a Messenger to come after me, whose name shall be Ahmad.'[1] But when he (Ahmad, i.e. Muhammad ﷺ) came to them with clear proofs, they said: 'This is plain magic.'"[2] (V. 61: 5,6)

"And who does more wrong than the one who invents a lie against Allâh, while he is being invited to Islam? And Allâh guides not the people who are Zâlimûn (polytheists, wrongdoers and disbelievers). They intend to put out the Light of Allâh (i.e. the religion of Islam, this Qur'ân, and Prophet Muhammad ﷺ) with

---

And there was also revealed: "O 'Ibâdî (My slaves) who have transgressed against themselves (by committing evil deeds and sins)! Despair not of the Mercy of Allâh." (V.39:53) (Sahih Al-Bukhari, Hadîth No. 4810)

[1] i.e. the second name of Prophet Muhammad ﷺ and it (Ahmad) literally means: "One who praises Allâh more than others."

[2] Narrated Jubair bin Mut'im ﷺ: Allâh's Messenger ﷺ said, "I have five names: I am Muhammad and Ahmad; I am Al-Mahî through whom Allâh will eliminate Al-Kufr (infidelity); I am Al-Hâshir who will be the first to be resurrected, the people being resurrected thereafter; and I am also Al-'Âqîb (i.e. there will be no Prophet after me)." (Sahih Al-Bukhari, Hadîth No. 3532)

their mouths. But Allâh will bring His Light to perfection even though the disbelievers hate (it). He it is Who has sent His Messenger (Muhammad ﷺ) with guidance and the religion of truth (Islamic Monotheism) to make it victorious over all (other) religions even though the *Mushrikûn* (polytheists, pagans, idolaters, and disbelievers in the Oneness of Allâh and in His Messenger Muhammad ﷺ) hate (it)." (V. 61: 7-9)

The Best Trade

"O you who believe! Shall I guide you to a trade that will save you from a painful torment? That you believe in Allâh and His Messenger (Muhammad ﷺ), and that you strive hard and fight in the Cause of Allâh with your wealth and your lives, that will be better for you, if you but know! (If you do so) He will forgive you your sins, and admit you into Gardens under which rivers flow, and pleasant dwellings in *'Adn* (Eden) Paradise; that is indeed the great success. And also (He will give you) another (blessing) which you love, help from Allâh (against your enemies) and a near victory. And give glad tidings (O Muhammad ﷺ) to the believers." (V.61: 10-13)

"O you who believe! Be you helpers (in the cause) of Allâh as said Isâ (Jesus), son of Maryam (Mary), to the *Hawârîyyûn* (the disciples): "Who are my helpers (in the Cause) of Allâh?" The *Hawârîyyûn* (the disciples) said: 'We are Allâh's helpers' (i.e. we will strive in His Cause!). Then a group of the Children of Israel believed and a group disbelieved. So, We gave power to those who believed against their enemies, and they became the victorious (uppermost).'" (V. 61: 14)

Who are the mischief-walkers

"And of mankind there is he whose speech may please you (O Muhammad ﷺ) in this worldly life, and he calls Allâh to witness as to that which is in his heart, yet he is the most quarrelsome of the opponents.[1] And when he turns away (from you O

---

[1] (a) Narrated 'Aishah رضى الله عنها: The Prophet ﷺ said, "The most hated person to Allâh is the one who is most quarrelsome of the opponents." (*Sahih*

Muhammad ﷺ), his effort in the land is to make mischief therein and to destroy the crops and the cattle, and Allâh likes not mischief. And when it is said to him, 'Fear Allâh,' he is led by arrogance to (more) crime. So, enough for him is Hell, and worst indeed is that place to rest!" (V. 2: 204-206)

Satan is a plain enemy

"And of mankind is he who would sell himself, seeking the Pleasure of Allâh. And Allâh is full of kindness to (His) slaves. O you who believe! Enter perfectly into Islam (by obeying all the rules and regulations of the religion of Islam) and follow not the footsteps of *Shaitân* (Satan). Verily, he is to you a plain enemy. Then if you slide back after the clear signs (Prophet Muhammad ﷺ, and this Qur'ân and Islam) have come to you, then know that Allâh is All-Mighty, All-Wise." (V. 2: 207-209)

"Do they then wait for anything other than that Allâh should come to them in the shadows of the clouds and the angels? (Then) the case would be already judged. And to Allâh return all matters (for decision). Ask the Children of Israel how many clear *Ayât* (proofs, evidences, verses, lessons, signs, revelations, etc.) We gave them. And whoever changes Allâh's Favor after it has come to him, [e.g. renounces the religion of Allâh (Islam) and accepts *Kufr* (disbelief)] then surely Allâh is Severe in punishment." (V. 2: 210,211)

"Beautified is the life of this world for those who disbelieve, and they mock at those who believe. But those who obey Allâh's Orders and keep away from what He has forbidden, will be above them on the Day of Resurrection. And Allâh gives (of His Bounty,

---

Al-Bukhâri, Hadîth No. 2457)

(b) Narrated Abu Umamah ﷺ: Allâh's Messenger ﷺ said: "(a) I guarantee a home in Paradise for a person who gives up arguments and disputes even if he is on the truth. (b) And [I (also) guarantee] a home in the middle of Paradise for a person who gives up lying (false statements) even while joking. (c) And [I (also) guarantee] a home in the highest part of Paradise for a person who has a high standard of character." (This *Hadith* is quoted by *Abu Dâwûd, At-Tirmidhi, An-Nasa'i* and *Ibn Majah*)

Blessings, Favors, and Honors on the Day of Resurrection) to whom He wills without limit." (V. 2: 212)

Mankind was one community

"Mankind was one community and Allâh sent Prophets with glad tidings and warnings, and with them He sent down the Scripture in truth to judge between people in matters wherein they differed. And only those to whom (the Scripture) was given differed concerning it after clear proofs had come unto them through hatred, one to another. Then Allâh by His Leave guided those who believed to the truth of that wherein they differed. And Allâh guides whom He wills to the Straight Path." (V. 2: 213)

Trials of the World

"Or think you that you will enter Paradise without such (trials) as came to those who passed away before you? They were afflicted with severe poverty and ailments and were so shaken that even the Messenger and those who believed along with him said, 'When (will come) the Help of Allâh?' Yes! Certainly, the Help of Allâh is near!" (V. 2: 214)

About the forbidden things

"O you who believe! Intoxicants (all kinds of alcoholic drinks), and gambling, and Al-Ansâb,[1] and Al-Azlâm (arrows for seeking luck or decision) are abominations of Shaitân's (Satan's)

---

[1] Animals that are sacrificed (slaughtered) on An-Nusub* and for the idols.

Narrated 'Abdullâh ﷺ: Allâh's Messenger ﷺ said that he met Zaid bin 'Amr bin Nufail at a place near Baldah and this had happened before Allâh's Messenger ﷺ received the Divine Revelation. Allâh's Messenger ﷺ presented a dish of meat (that had been offered to him by the pagans) to Zaid bin 'Amr, but Zaid refused to eat of it and then said (to the pagans), "I do not eat of what you have sacrificed (slaughtered) on your stone-altars (Ansâb) nor do I eat except that on which Allâh's Name has been mentioned on slaughtering." (Sahih Al-Bukhâri, Hadîth No. 5499)

* An-Nusub were stone-altars at fixed places or graves, whereon sacrifices were slaughtered on certain occasions in the name of idols, jinn, angels, pious men, saints, in order to honor them, or to expect some benefit from them.

handiwork. So, avoid (strictly all) that (abominations) in order that you may be successful.[1] *Shaitân* (Satan) wants only to excite enmity and hatred between you with intoxicants (alcoholic drinks) and gambling, and hinder you from the remembrance of Allâh and from *As-Salât* (the prayer). So, will you not then abstain? And obey Allâh and the Messenger (Muhammad ﷺ), and beware (of even coming near to drinking[2] or gambling or *Al-Ansâb*, or *Al-Azlâm*) and fear Allâh. Then if you turn away, you should know that it is Our Messenger's duty to convey (the Message) in the clearest way." (V. 5: 90-92)

Do good deeds with Perfection

"Those who believe and do righteous good deeds, there is no sin on them for what they ate (in the past), if they fear Allâh (by keeping away from things forbidden by Him), and believe and do righteous good deeds, and again fear Allâh and believe, and once

---

[1] What is said regarding the one who regards an alcoholic drink lawful to drink, and calls it by another name.

Narrated Abu 'Âmir or Abu Mâlik Al-Ash'ari that he heard the Prophet ﷺ saying, "From among my followers there will be some people who will consider illegal sexual intercourse, the wearing of silk, the drinking of alcoholic drinks, and the use of musical instruments as lawful. And (from them), there will be some who will stay near the side of a mountain, and in the evening their shepherd will come to them with their sheep and ask them for something, but they will say to him, 'Return to us tomorrow.' Allâh will destroy them during the night and will let the mountain fall on them, and He will transform the rest of them into monkeys and pigs and they will remain so till the Day of Resurrection." (*Sahih Al-Bukhâri, Hadîth* No. 5590)

[2] a) Narrated Ibn 'Umar رضى الله عنهما: Allâh's Messenger ﷺ said, "Whoever drinks alcoholic drinks in this world and does not repent (i.e. stops drinking alcoholic drinks, and begs Allâh to forgive him before his death) will be deprived of it in the Hereafter." (*Sahih Al-Bukhâri, Hadîth* No. 5575)

b) Narrated Anas ﷺ: I heard from Allâh's Messenger ﷺ a narration which none other than I will narrate to you. The Prophet ﷺ said, "From among the portents of the Hour are the following: General ignorance (in religious affairs) will prevail, (religious) knowledge will decrease, illegal sexual intercourse will prevail, alcoholic drinks will be drunk (in abundance), men will decrease and women will increase so much so that for every fifty women there will be one again fear Allâh and do good deeds with *Ihsân* (perfection). And Allâh loves the good-doers." (V. 5: 93)

No distinction between the Messengers

"And those who believe in Allâh and His Messengers and make no distinction between any of them (Messengers), We shall give them their rewards; and Allâh is Ever Oft-Forgiving, Most Merciful." (V. 4: 152)

About Moses

"The people of the Scripture (Jews) ask you to cause a book to descend upon them from heaven. Indeed, they asked Mûsâ (Moses) for even greater than that, when they said: 'Show us Allâh in public,' but they were struck with thunderclap and lightning for their wickedness. Then they worshipped the calf even after clear proofs, evidences, and signs had come to them. (Even) so We forgave them. And We gave Mûsâ (Moses) a clear proof of authority." (V. 4: 153)

"And for (breaking) their covenant, We raised over them the Mount and (on the other occasion) We said to them: 'Enter the gate prostrating (or bowing) with humility;' and We commanded them: 'Transgress not (by doing worldly works) on the Sabbath (Saturday).' And We took from them a firm covenant. Because of their breaking the covenant, and of their rejecting the *Ayât* (proofs, evidences, verses, lessons, signs, revelations, etc.) of

---

man to look after them." (*Sahih Al-Bukhâri, Hadîth* No. 5577)

c) Narrated Abu Hurairah ﷺ: The Prophet ﷺ said, "An adulterer-fornicator at the time he is committing illegal sexual intercourse is not a believer; and a person, at the time of drinking an alcoholic drink is not a believer; and a thief, at the time of stealing is not a believer."

Ibn Shihâb said: 'Abdul-Mâlik bin Abu Bakr bin 'Abdur-Rahmân bin Al-Hârith bin Hishâm told me that Abu Bakr ﷺ used to narrate that narration to him on the authority of Abu Hurairah ﷺ. He used to add that Abu Bakr ﷺ used to mention, besides the above cases: "And he who robs (takes illegally something by force) while the people are looking at him, is not a believer at the time he is robbing (taking it)." (*Sahih Al-Bukhâri, Hadîth* No. 5578)

Allâh, and of their killing the Prophets unjustly, and of their saying: 'Our hearts are wrapped (with coverings, i.e. we do not understand what the Messengers say),' – nay, Allâh has set a seal upon their hearts because of their disbelief, so they believe not but a little." (V. 4: 154,155)

False charge of Jews against Mary

"And because of their (Jews) disbelief and uttering against Maryam (Mary عليها السلام) a grave false charge (that she has committed illegal sexual intercourse); And because of their saying (in boast), 'We killed Messiah 'Îsâ (Jesus), son of Maryam (Mary), the Messenger of Allâh,' – but they killed him not, nor crucified him, but it appeared so to them [the resemblance of 'Îsâ (Jesus) was put over another man (and they killed that man)], and those who differ therein are full of doubts. They have no (certain) knowledge, they follow nothing but conjecture. For surely they killed him not [i.e. 'Îsâ (Jesus), son of Maryam (Mary) عليهما السلام]. But Allâh raised him ['Îsâ (Jesus)] up (with his body and soul) unto Himself (and he عليه السلام is in the heavens). And Allâh is Ever All-Powerful, All-Wise." (V. 4: 156-158)

"And there is none of the people of the Scripture (Jews and Christians) but must believe in him ['Îsâ (Jesus), son of Maryam (Mary), as only a Messenger of Allâh and a human being][1] before his

---

[1] The advent (descent) of 'Îsâ (Jesus), [son of Maryam (Mary)] ﷺ.

a) Narrated Abu Hurairah ﷺ: Allâh's Messenger ﷺ said, "By Him in Whose Hand my soul is, surely ['Îsâ (Jesus)], the son of Maryam (Mary) عليهما السلام will shortly descend amongst you (Muslims), and will judge mankind justly by the law of the Qur'ân (as a just ruler); he will break the Cross and kill the pigs and there will be no Jîzyah* (i.e. taxation taken from non-Muslims). Money will be in abundance so that nobody will accept it, and a single prostration to Allâh (in prayer) will be better than the whole world and whatever is in it." Abu Hurairah ﷺ added: "If you wish, you can recite (this Verse of the Qur'ân): "And there is none of the people of the Scripture (Jews and Christians) but must believe in him [i.e. 'Îsâ (Jesus) عليه السلام as a Messenger of Allâh and a human being] before his ['Îsâ (Jesus) عليه السلام or a

['Îsâ (Jesus) عليه السلام or a Jew's or a Christian's] death[1] (at the time of the appearance of the angel of death). And on the Day of Resurrection, he ['Îsâ (Jesus)] will be a witness against them." (V. 4: 159)

For the wrongdoing of the Jews

"For the wrongdoing of the Jews, We made unlawful for them certain good foods which had been lawful for them – and for their hindering many from Allâh's way. And their taking of Ribâ[2] (usury) though they were forbidden from taking it and their devouring of men's substance wrongfully (bribery). And We have prepared for the disbelievers among them a painful torment. But those among them who are well-grounded in knowledge, and the believers, believe in what has been sent down to you (Muhammad ﷺ) and what was sent down before you; and those who perform As-Salât (Iqâmat-as-Salât – prayer), and give Zakât (obligatory charity) and believe in Allâh and in the Last Day, it is they to whom We shall give a great reward." (V. 4: 160-162)

Jew's or Christian's] death, and on the Day of Resurrection, he ['Îsâ (Jesus) عليه السلام] will be a witness against them." (4:159)

(See Fath Al-Bari) According to the quotation of Kushmaihani there is the word Al-Jizyah instead of Al-Harb. (Sahih Al-Bukhâri, Hadîth No. 3448)

b) Narrated Abu Hurairah ؓ Allâh's Messenger ﷺ said: "How will you be when the son of Maryam (Mary) [i.e. 'Îsâ (Jesus) عليه السلام] descends amongst you, and he will judge people by the law of the Qur'ân and not by the law of the Injeel (Gospel)." (Fath Al-Bari, Vol. 7, Pages 304 and 305) (Sahih Al-Bukhâri, Hadîth No. 3449)

* The Jîzyah: a tax imposed on non-Muslims (who would keep their own religion, rather than embrace Islam) will not be accepted by 'Îsâ (Jesus) ﷺ, but all people will be required to embrace Islam and there will be no other alternative.

[1] "Before his death," has two interpretations: before Jesus' death after his descent from the heavens, or a Jew's or a Christian's death, at the time of the appearance of the Angel of Death when he will realize that 'Îsâ (Jesus) was only a Messenger of Allâh, and had no share in Divinity.

[2] Ribâ: Usury, which is of two major kinds: (a) Riba Nasî'ah, i.e., interest on lent money; (b) Riba Fadl, i.e., taking a superior thing of the same kind of goods by giving more of the same kind of goods of inferior quality, e.g., dates of superior quality for dates of inferior quality in greater amount. Islam strictly forbids all kinds of usury.

About Revelation to the Messengers

"Verily, We have sent the Revelation to you (O Muhammad ﷺ) as We sent the Revelation to Nûh (Noah) and the Prophets after him; We (also) sent the Revelation to Ibrâhîm (Abraham), Ismâ'îl (Ishmael), Ishâq (Isaac), Ya'qûb (Jacob), and Al-Asbât [the offspring of the twelve sons of Ya'qûb (Jacob)], 'Îsâ (Jesus), Ayyub (Job), Yûnus (Jonah), Hârûn (Aaron), and Sulaimân (Solomon); and to Dâwûd (David) We gave the Zabûr (Psalms). And Messengers We have mentioned to you before, and Messengers We have not mentioned to you, – and to Mûsâ (Moses) Allâh spoke directly. Messengers as bearers of good news as well as of warning in order that mankind should have no plea against Allâh after the (coming of) Messengers. And Allâh is Ever All-Powerful, All-Wise." (V. 4: 163-165)

"But Allâh bears witness to that which He has sent down (the Qur'ân) unto you (O Muhammad ﷺ); He has sent it down with His Knowledge, and the angels bear witness. "And Allâh is All-Sufficient as a Witness." (V.4: 166)

About those who disbelieve

"Verily, those who disbelieve [by concealing the truth about Prophet Muhammad ﷺ and his message of true Islamic Monotheism written in the Taurât (Torah) and the Injeel (Gospel) with them] and prevent (mankind) from the path of Allâh (Islamic Monotheism); they have certainly strayed far away. (Tafsir Al-Qurtubî). Verily, those who disbelieve and did wrong [by concealing the truth about Prophet Muhammad ﷺ and his message of true Islamic Monotheism written in the Taurât (Torah) and the Injeel (Gospel) with them]; Allâh will not forgive them, nor will He guide them to any way – (Tafsir Al-Qurtubî) Except the way of Hell, to dwell therein forever; and this is ever easy for Allâh." [1] (V. 4: 167-169)

---

[1] a) It is obligatory to have belief in the Messengership of the Prophet (Muhammad ﷺ). Narrated Abu Hurairah ﷺ: Allâh's Messenger ﷺ said: "By Him (Allâh) in Whose Hand Muhammad's soul is, there is none from

"O mankind! Verily, there has come to you the Messenger (Muhammad ﷺ) with the truth from your Lord. So believe in him, it is better for you. But if you disbelieve, then certainly to Allâh belongs all that is in the heavens and the earth. And Allâh is Ever All-Knowing, All-Wise." (V. 4: 170)

A Message to the Christians

"O people of the Scripture (Christians)! Do not exceed the limits in your religion, nor say of Allâh aught but the truth. The Messiah 'Îsâ (Jesus), son of Maryam (Mary), was (no more than) a Messenger of Allâh and His Word, ("Be!" – and he was) which He bestowed on

---

amongst the Jews and the Christians (of these present nations) who hears about me and then dies without believing in the Message with which I have been sent (i.e. Islâmic Monotheism), but he will be from the dwellers of the (Hell) Fire." (*Sahih Muslim*, the Book of Faith, Vol.1, *Hadith* No. 240)

b) The asking of (angel) Jibrîl (Gabriel) from the Prophet ﷺ about Belief, Islâm, *Ihsân* (perfection) and the knowledge of the Hour (Doomsday), and their explanation given to him by the Prophet ﷺ. Then the Prophet ﷺ said (to his Companions): "Jibrîl (Gabriel) عليه السلام came to teach you your religion." So the Prophet ﷺ regarded all that as a religion. And all that which the Prophet ﷺ explained to the delegation of 'Abdûl-Qais was a part of Faith. (See *Sahih Al-Bukhâri*, *Hadîth* No.53 and 87) And the Statement of Allâh : "And whoever seeks a religion other than Islâm, it will never be accepted of him." (V. 3:85)

Narrated Abu Hurairah ﷺ: One day while the Prophet ﷺ was sitting in the company of some people, a man came and asked, "What is Faith?" Allâh's Messenger ﷺ replied, "Faith is to believe in Allâh, His angels, (the) Meeting with Him, His Messengers, and to believe in Resurrection."* Then he further asked, "What is Islâm?" Allâh's Messenger ﷺ replied, "To worship Allâh Alone and none else, to perform As-Salât (Iqamât-as-Salât) prayer, to give the Zakât (obligatory charity) and to observe Saum (fasts) during the month of Ramadân,"** then he further asked, "What is Ihsân (perfection)?" Allâh's Messenger ﷺ replied, "To worship Allâh as if you see Him, and if you cannot achieve this state of devotion then you must consider that He is looking at you." Then he further asked, "When will the Hour be established?" Allâh's Messenger ﷺ replied, "The answerer has no better knowledge than the questioner. But I will inform you about its portents:

(1) When a slave (lady) gives birth to her master.

Maryam (Mary) and a spirit (*Rûh*)[1] created by Him; so believe in Allâh and His Messengers. Say not: 'Three (trinity)!' Cease! (it is) better for you. For Allâh is (the only) One *Ilâh* (God), Glorified is He (Far Exalted is He) above having a son. To Him belongs all that is in

---

(2) When the shepherds of black camels start boasting and competing with others in the construction of higher buildings. And the Hour is one of the five things which nobody knows except Allâh."

The Prophet ﷺ then recited: "Verily, the knowledge of the Hour is with Allâh (Alone)." (V. 31:34). Then that man left and the Prophet ﷺ asked his Companions to call him back, but they could not see him. Then the Prophet ﷺ said, "That was (angel) Jibrâîl (Gabriel عليه السلام) who came to teach the people their religion."

Abu 'Abdullâh ﷺ said: He (the Prophet ﷺ) considered all that as a part of Faith. (*Sahih Al-Bukhâri, Hadîth* No.50).

* In this *Hadîth*, only 4 articles are mentioned, while in another *Hadîth*, 6 articles are mentioned: (i) Allâh, (ii) His Angels, (iii) His Books (the Torah, the Gospel, the Qur'ân and all the other Holy Books revealed by Allâh), (iv) His Messengers, (v) Day of Resurrection and (vi) *Al-Qadar* (Divine Preordainments), i.e. whatever Allâh has ordained, must come to pass.

** Again the principles of Islâm mentioned here are 4, but in other narrations, they are 5 – 5th is the pilgrimage (*Hajj*) to Makkah for the one who can afford it once in a lifetime.

[1] *Rûh-ullâh*: According to the early religious scholars from among the Companions of the Prophet ﷺ and their students and the *Mujtahidûn*, there is a rule to distinguish between the two nouns in the genitive construction:

a) When one of the two nouns is Allâh, and the other is a person or a thing, e.g. Allâh's House (*Bait-ullâh*); Allâh's Messenger (*Rasûl-ullâh*); and Allâh's slave ('*Abdullâh*); Allâh's spirit (*Rûh-ullâh*), the rule for the above words is that the second noun, e.g., house, messenger, slave or spirit is created by Allâh and is honorable with Him, and similarly, Allâh's spirit may be understood as the spirit of Allâh, in fact it is a soul created by Allâh, i.e. 'Îsâ (Jesus). And it was His Word: "Be!" – and he was [i.e. 'Îsâ (Jesus) was created like Adam].

b) But when one of the two is Allâh and the second is neither a person nor a thing, then it is not a created thing but is a quality of Allâh, e.g. Allâh's Knowledge ('*Ilm-ullâh*); Allâh's Life (*Hayât-ullâh*); Allâh's Statement (*Kalâm-ullâh*); and Allâh's Self (*Dhat-ullâh*).

the heavens and all that is in the earth. And Allâh is All-Sufficient as a Disposer of affairs.[1] The Messiah will never be proud to reject to be a slave of Allâh, nor the angels who are the near (to Allâh). And whosoever rejects His worship and is proud, then He will gather them all together unto Himself." (V. 4:171,172)

"So, as for those who believed (in the Oneness of Allâh – Islamic Monotheism) and did deeds of righteousness, He will give them their (due) rewards – and more out of His Bounty. But as for those who refused His worship and were proud, He will punish them with a painful torment. And they will not find for themselves besides Allâh any protector or helper." (V. 4: 173)

"O mankind! Verily, there has come to you a convincing proof (Prophet Muhammad ﷺ) from your Lord; and We sent down to you a manifest light (this Qur'ân). So, as for those who believed in Allâh and held fast to Him, He will admit them to His Mercy and Grace (i.e. Paradise), and guide them to Himself by the Straight Path." (V. 4: 174, 175)

Those who ridicule the Truth

"Lest a person should say: 'Alas, my grief that I was undutiful to Allâh (i.e. I have not done what Allâh has ordered me to do), and I was indeed among those who mocked [at the truth! i.e. Lâ ilâha illallâh (none has the right to be worshipped but Allâh), the Qur'ân, and Muhammad ﷺ and at the faithful believers].' Or (lest) he should say: 'If only Allâh had guided me, I should indeed have been among the Muttaqûn [the pious believers of Islamic Monotheism who fear

---

[1] Narrated 'Ubadah ﷺ: The Prophet ﷺ said, "If anyone testifies that Lâ ilâha illallâh (none has the right to be worshipped but Allâh Alone) Who has no partners, and that Muhammad is His slave and His Messenger, and that Jesus عليه السلام is Allâh's slave and His Messenger and His Word ("Be!" – and he was) which He bestowed on Mary and a spirit (Rûh) created by Him, and that Paradise is the truth, and Hell is the truth – Allâh will admit him into Paradise with the deeds which he had done even if those deeds were few." (Junadah, the subnarrator said, "'Ubâdah added: 'Such a person can enter Paradise through any of its eight gates he likes.'") (Sahih Al-Bukhâri, Hadîth No. 3435)

Allâh much (abstain from all kinds of sins and evil deeds which He has forbidden) and love Allâh much (perform all kinds of good deeds which He has ordained)].' Or (lest) he should say when he sees the torment: 'If only I had another chance (to return to the world), then I should indeed be among the *Muhsinûn* (good-doers – who perform good deeds totally for Allâh's sake only without any show-off or to gain praise or fame, and in accordance with the *Sunnah* of Allâh's Messenger Muhammad ﷺ).'" (V. 39: 56-58)

"Yes! Verily, there came to you My *Ayât* (proofs, evidences, verses, lessons, signs, revelations, etc.) and you denied them, and were proud[1] and were among the disbelievers. And on the Day of Resurrection you will see those who lied against Allâh (i.e. attributed to Him sons, partners) – their faces will be black. Is there not in Hell an abode for the arrogant?" (V. 39: 59,60)

About those who are pious

"And Allâh will deliver those who are the *Muttaqûn* [the pious believers of Islamic Monotheism who fear Allâh much (abstain from all kinds of sins and evil deeds which He has forbidden) and love Allâh much (perform all kinds of good deeds which He has ordained)] to their places of success (Paradise). Evil shall touch them not, nor shall they grieve. Allâh is the Creator of all things, and He is the *Wakîl* (Trustee, Disposer of affairs, Guardian) over all things. To Him belong the keys of the heavens and the earth. And those who disbelieve in the *Ayât* (proofs, evidences, verses, signs, revelations, etc.) of Allâh, such are they who will be the losers." (V. 39: 61-63)

---

[1]   Narrated Abdullah bin Mas'ûd ﵂: Allâh's Messenger ﷺ said, "Whosoever has pride in his heart equal to the weight of an atom (or a small ant) shall not enter Paradise." A person (amongst the audience) said, "Verily, a person loves that his dress should be beautiful, and his shoes should be beautiful." The Prophet ﷺ remarked, "Verily, Allâh is the Most Beautiful and He loves beauty. Pride is to completely disregard the truth, and to scorn (to look down upon) the people." (*Sahih Muslim*, Book of Faith, Vol. 1, *Hadîth* No. 164)

Worship is for the only One

"Say (O Muhammad ﷺ to the polytheists): "Do you order me to worship other than Allâh? O you fools!" And indeed it has been revealed to you (O Muhammad ﷺ), as it was to those (Allâh's Messengers) before you: "If you join others in worship with Allâh, (then) surely, (all) your deeds will be in vain, and you will certainly be among the losers."[1] Nay! But worship Allâh (Alone and none else), and be among the grateful." (V. 39:64-66)

"They made not a just estimate of Allâh such as is due to Him. "And on the Day of Resurrection the whole of the earth will be grasped by His Hand[2] and the heavens will be rolled up in His Right Hand. Glorified is He, and Exalted is He above all that they associate as partners with Him! And the Trumpet will be blown, and all who are in the heavens and all who are on the earth will swoon away, except him whom Allâh wills. Then it will be blown a second time, and behold they will be standing, looking on

---

[1] a) Narrated 'Abdullâh ﷺ: The Prophet ﷺ said one statement and I said another. The Prophet ﷺ said: "Whoever dies while still invoking anything other than Allâh as a rival to Allâh, will enter Hell (Fire)." And I said, "Whoever dies without invoking anything as a rival to Allâh, will enter Paradise." (Sahih Al-Bukhâri, Hadîth No. 4497)

b) Narrated Anas ﷺ: The Prophet ﷺ was asked about the great sins. He said, "They are:

    a) To join others in worship with Allâh.

    b) To be undutiful to one's parents.

    c) To kill a person (which Allâh has forbidden to be killed, i.e., to commit the crime of murdering).

    d) And to give a false witness." (Sahih Al-Bukhâri, Hadîth No. 2653)

[2] Narrated Abû Hurairah ﷺ: I heard Allâh's Messenger ﷺ saying, "(On the Day of Resurrection) Allâh will grasp the whole planet of earth (by His Hand), and roll all the heavens up with His Right Hand, and then He will say, 'I am the King; where are the kings of the earth?'" (Sahih Al-Bukhari, Hadîth No. 4812)

[3] a) Narrated Abû Hurairah ﷺ: The Prophet ﷺ said, "I will be the first to raise my head after the second blowing of the Trumpet and will see Mûsâ (Moses) holding or clinging to the Throne; and I will not know whether he had been in that state all the time or after the blowing of the Trumpet." (Sahih Al-Bukhari, Hadîth No. 4813)

(waiting)." [3] (V. 39: 67,68)

"And the earth will shine with the light of its Lord (Allâh, when He will come to judge among men), and the Book will be placed (open), and the Prophets and the witnesses will be brought forward, and it will be judged between them with truth, and they will not be wronged. And each person will be paid in full of what he did; and He is Best Aware of what they do." (V.39: 69, 70)

About Hell and Paradise

"And those who disbelieved will be driven to Hell in groups till when they reach it, the gates thereof will be opened (suddenly like a prison at the arrival of the prisoners). And its keepers will say: 'Did not the Messengers come to you from yourselves, reciting to you the Verses of your Lord, and warning you of the Meeting of this Day of yours?' They will say: 'Yes,' but the Word of torment has been justified against the disbelievers! It will be said (to them): 'Enter you the gates of Hell to abide therein. And (indeed) what an evil abode of the arrogant!'" (V. 39: 71,72)

"And those who kept their duty to their Lord (Al-Mutaqûn)[1] will be led to Paradise in groups till when they reach it, and its gates will be opened (before their arrival for their reception) and its keepers will say: Salâmun 'Alaikum (peace be upon you)! You have done well, so enter here to abide therein forever.' And they will say: 'All praise and thanks are Allâh's Who has fulfilled His Promise to us and has made us inherit (this) land. We can dwell in

---

b) Narrated Abû Hurairah ◈: The Prophet ﷺ said, "Between the two blowings of the Trumpet there will be forty." The people said, "O Abû Hurairah (◈)! Forty days?" I refused to reply. They said, "Forty years?" I refused to reply. They said, "Forty months?" I refused to reply and added: Everything of a human body will waste away, perish or decay except the last coccyx bone (of the tail) and from that bone Allâh will reconstruct the whole body. (Sahih Al-Bukhari, Hadîth No. 4814)

[1] The pious believers of Islamic Monotheism who fear Allâh much (abstain from all kinds of sins and evil deeds which He has forbidden) and love Allâh much (perform all kinds of good deeds which He has ordained).

Paradise where we will; how excellent a reward for the (pious, good) workers!' And you will see the angels surrounding the Throne (of Allâh) from all round, glorifying the praises of their Lord (Allâh). And they (all the creatures) will be judged with truth. And it will be said, 'All praise and thanks are Allâh's, the Lord of the 'Âlamîn (mankind, jinn and all that exists).'" (V. 39:73-75)

❀❀❀

This religion, Islam is a heavenly system (or regime) for all the dwellers of the earth, and it is a mighty treasure if only mankind realizes its authenticity and truth. And in what a great need the whole world is today for real understanding and thorough studying of its rules and regulations – i.e. the Noble Qur'ân and the pious *Sunnah* (legal ways, etc.) of the Prophet Muhammad ﷺ as these (the Qur'ân and *As-Sunnah*) accede to the demand of the people to know their Creator (the Almighty Allâh, the Blessed, the Most High), organize and regulate the relations between them on the foundations of (Godly) Divine Justice and equality and respond to the human nature equally to that which makes sure for them their welfare (happiness) in this world and in the Hereafter (after their deaths).

And how many disasters, calamities and wars, the mankind of the whole world is suffering because of their differences in their faith, and organizations, which have broken them into the worst type of breaking, so there remains no way out for any security or any safety or any peace except with Islam, i.e., by putting in practice the Laws of their Creator, Allâh, (i.e., the Qur'ân and *As-Sunnah*).

Invitation to this Islam is incumbent upon all those who have known it, and have enjoyed its taste and have been guided through its guidance. In fact, it is a great responsibility and a trust (of Allâh) over (the shoulders of) all those who know Islam, to preach it to mankind and invite them to it in a language which they speak and understand.

To end the story, we invoke Allâh to guide mankind on the right path, and to save them from the afflictions and trials, and also save them from the Hell-fire. We send our *Salat* (Allâh's blessings) and *Salam* (greetings) to our Prophet Muhammad ﷺ.

Islam is the religion that Allâh has chosen for mankind. He said:

"Truly, the religion with Allâh is Islam. Those who were given the Scripture (Jews and Christians) did not differ except out of mutual jealousy, after knowledge had come to them. And whoever disbelieves in the *Ayât* (proofs, evidences, verses, signs, revelations, etc.) of Allâh, then surely Allâh is Swift in calling to account." (V. 3:19)

This means that the message is universal. Due to this fact, man does not need to develop or devise new laws to suit every age and life style. It is a way of life that affects every aspect of man's life, the social, the political, the economic, etc. Islam has a solution to every problem regardless of its nature and gravity. It is a Divine message, which Allâh chose Muhammad ﷺ to convey to mankind. To man, He also revealed the Qur'ân, His last Book which comprises an unalterable constitution.

Now that you have read this booklet and become more acquainted with the central principles of Islam, it is up to you to make the choice. As Allâh says:

"Verily, We showed him the way, whether he be grateful or ungrateful. Verily, We have prepared for the disbelievers iron chains, iron collars, and a blazing Fire. Verily, the *Abrâr* (the pious – believers of Islamic Monotheism) shall drink of a cup (of wine) mixed with (water from a spring in Paradise called) *Kâfûr*." (V. 76: 3-5)

Allâh is so Merciful and far removed from injustice that He says:

"We never punish until We have sent a Messenger (to give warning)." (V. 17:15)

Out of our concern for you, we have prepared for you this message. "Truly, the religion with Allâh is Islam. Those who were given the Scripture (Jews and Christians) did not differ except, out of mutual jealousy, after knowledge had come to them. And whoever disbelieves in the *Ayât* (proofs, evidences, verses, signs, revelations, etc.) of Allâh, then surely, Allâh is Swift in calling to account." (V. 3:19)

And He (🕮) said:

"This day, I have perfected your religion for you, completed My Favour upon you, and have chosen for you Islam as your religion. But as for him who is forced by severe hunger, with no inclination to sin (such can eat these above mentioned meats), then surely, Allâh is Oft-Forgiving, Most Merciful." (V. 5:3)